Compost

Thanks to Anna Hofny-Collins for her help in the early stages of this book, and to Christopher Leach, Antonia Williams, Dean Riddle and Tom Dawson for their enthusiastic participation. Thank you also to Camilla Stoddart who has been supportive and encouraging, and to Mat, who I couldn't have done without.

Compost

Clare Foster

CASSELL ILLUSTRATED

The right of Clare Foster to be identified as the author of this work
has been asserted by her in accordance with the Copyright,
Designs and Patents Act 1988.

First published in Great Britain in 2002 by
Cassell Illustrated
2–4 Heron Quays, London E14 4JP
A division of the Octopus Publishing Group

A CIP catalogue record for this book is available
from the British Library

ISBN 0 304 36231 X

Designer: Justin Hunt
Commissioning Editor: Camilla Stoddart
Illustrator: John Woodcock

Printed in Slovenia

Contents

Introduction

In this convenience-driven, supermarket-ridden world, we may not feel very connected to the soil but, like it or not, every one of us depends on it. It is the crucial link in the human food chain: without it we would not survive. Compost provides us with a way of caring for the soil, putting back the goodness that is taken out when we cultivate the land. For a gardener, compost has enormous benefits, improving the quality of the soil, plants and crops.

The most important thing about compost, however, is that it is good for the environment: it is the most effective way of recycling organic waste. British people generate 28 million tonnes of household waste each year, while in North America, the figure is closer to 200 million tonnes. Alarmingly, most of this waste ends up in landfill sites and recycling rates are shamefully low (only about 10 percent in Britain and 30 percent in the USA). Recycling organic waste is one of the ways we can make a positive contribution to the environment. It may not seem much, but this so-called 'green' waste makes up a third to a half of an average household's total rubbish. If organic matter isn't recycled, it goes off to the landfill site and when it is mixed with other rubbish, its normal decomposition cycle can't occur. Instead, it forms a putrid mess that emits methane, a damaging greenhouse gas. Worse, this substance can mix with other industrial wastes, leaching into the soil and polluting rivers. This, and the sheer volume of waste arising, constitutes a severe problem. How long can we continue like this?

Anyone can make compost. Whether you have a large country garden, a small city courtyard, a fifth-floor balcony, or even no garden at all, you can find a way that will suit you – and if you don't need the end result, why not give it to a gardening neighbour or to a community composting scheme? Making compost is not difficult and – despite many people's misconceptions – nor is it, or the end result, smelly, dirty or unhygienic. In reality, it is immensely rewarding to produce such a beneficial substance from materials that would otherwise have been thrown away. Composting is something to be enjoyed! It is a positive act and if more people did it, we'd be much closer to a safer, cleaner, greener world.

The basics

Composting is a practice that has been going on for thousands of years. In fact it is only in the last 150 years, with the introduction of artificial fertilizers, that many people have forgotten just how valuable a resource it is. Even in prehistoric times, it is likely that farmers caught on to the benefits of piling waste matter in a heap, perhaps noticing that plants grew better there. They put two and two together and started to use their decomposed rubbish in the cultivation of crops.

Wild plants grow prolifically on a heap of nutrient-rich decomposing matter.

The Romans certainly composted. The technique was recorded by the scholar Marcus Porcius Cato, who set out recommendations for farmers in his manuscript *De Agricultura*, a first-hand account of farming life in Italy more than 2,000 years ago. 'Be sure to have a big manure heap,' he advises (using 'manure' in the true sense of the word to mean 'fertilizer' rather than animal dung as many people understand it today). Cato listed the sources of this manure: animal bedding, lupin vines, chaff, bean vines, husks, holm oak and oak foliage.

Even William Shakespeare referred to compost in his most famous play: Hamlet, in a conversation with his mother, says: 'And do not spread the compost on the weeds to make them ranker.'

In the latter years of the Roman Empire, however, the practice of enriching the soil was neglected. Roman emperors donated farmland to favoured officials who sacked the farmers and used slaves to run the farms, exploiting the land by planting and harvesting but ignoring the fact that the soil's goodness needed to be replenished. Over time, the land became so run down that it could only be used for grazing cattle. Some people even claim that poor soil fertility was one of the contributing factors to the fall of the Roman Empire.

Learning from mistakes as well as successes, generation after generation continued to make and use compost to enrich the soil. There are references to composting in the Bible: Luke writes about a man who has a fig tree growing in his vineyard. He complains to his vine-dresser that the tree bears no fruit, and is advised to 'dig around it and manure it'. In Renaissance times, the writer and printer William Caxton wrote about the benefits of 'compostyng'. Even William Shakespeare referred to compost in his most famous play: Hamlet, in a conversation with his mother, says: 'And do not spread the compost on the weeds to make them ranker.'

It wasn't until the mid-nineteenth century, when industrialization resulted in the production of artificial fertilizers, pesticides and herbicides, that the need for compost lessened. Chemicals were pumped into the land by farmers. At first they didn't know that they were poisoning the soil, destroying some of the millions of insects, fungi and bacteria that keep it healthy. Gradually, however, people began to worry about the implications of such methods. A British agronomist and botanist, Sir Albert Howard, now hailed as the founder of the organic farming movement, began the backlash in the first half of the twentieth century. Between 1905 and 1939, Howard was based in India, where he carried out experiments on his 75-acre farm, ensuring that the soil was fed properly with compost and manure. He found that over a period of time, his crops became more resistant to disease. In turn, his cattle, strengthened by eating crops from a soil that was rich in organic matter and devoid of chemicals, also became more healthy. The ultimate test was when they came into contact with other cattle that had foot and mouth disease – none of Howard's cattle succumbed, proving that they had built up an

'Artificial fertilizers lead to artificial nutrition, artificial animals and finally to artificial men and women.' Albert Howard

immunity through their healthy diet. Later, Howard developed what is now known as the Indore process of composting (named after the area where he was stationed from 1924), which was based on an ideal of three parts plant matter to one part animal manure. The principles at the root of Howard's thinking are summed up in an unforgettable statement that we would all do well to remember: 'Artificial fertilizers lead to artificial nutrition, artificial animals and finally to artificial men and women.'

Being organic

In the United States, the organic movement was founded by J. J. Rodale who established the monthly publication Organic Farming and Gardening in 1942. In Britain, the beginning of the organic movement was marked by the formation of the Soil Association in 1946, by a pioneering woman farmer, Lady Eve Balfour. The principal concern of the Soil Association was the depletion of healthy soil through intensive farming systems and, in the early years, it was involved mainly with research and building its membership base. However, the organic movement remained marginal until the early 1970s, when the establishment of organisations such as Greenpeace and Friends of the Earth brought increased awareness of environmental issues. Another 15 years passed before organic food appeared on the supermarket shelves, bringing a new credibility to the movement, and in 1995 the British government initiated the Organic Aid Scheme to help organic farmers, broadening it further. Today, research is still going on as to whether organically grown crops are 'better for you' than those grown using artificial fertilizers and pesticides.

The Soil Association, at the forefront of this research, has carried out tests to prove that organic vegetables contain more vitamins than those grown inorganically, including the all-important phytonutrients that can help safeguard against diseases such as cancer.

As the demand for organic food increases, individuals are becoming more aware of the benefits of composting. Some have allotments or vegetable patches, where composting is carried out on almost every plot; others belong to community composting networks, which bring members of a neighbourhood together to pool resources and compost more efficiently on a larger scale. Even if you don't have a garden, you can help by separating out your organic waste to go into a centralized composting system. Local government is also getting involved. An increasing number of local authorities in Britain (currently about 50 percent) have set up these centralized schemes, either collecting green waste from the kerb or encouraging people to take it to civic amenity sites. The organic matter is then composted and the end product sold. The British government has introduced various schemes to encourage this sort of activity, including a landfill tax in 1996 and, more recently, a system of recycling credit payments to authorities and private companies that are actively promoting recycling. However, Britain is lagging behind other countries when it comes to such schemes. In the Netherlands, for example, the separation of organic waste at source is compulsory for all households. Different bins are provided for green waste, tin cans, glass, plastics, etc, all of which are collected from the home. In the United States, centralized composting is commonplace, and other types of organic waste are also recycled, including meats and fatty products, to produce compost that is sold into both gardening and agricultural markets. In some areas there is also an 'on farm' composting facility, where the farmer is paid a fee to receive and compost waste.

All these ideas can and will be developed in years to come, but in the meantime, us lowly gardeners can do our bit by stepping up the home composting. And believe me, it can become quite an obsession. There's something immensely satisfying about producing such a life-giving substance from materials that are perceived as waste, and once you get hooked you'll find that you're constantly trying to produce more, better quality compost.

What is compost?

I am an organic gardener, so making compost is central to my way of gardening. I admit that I don't feel very glamorous cycling to my vegetable patch on my allotment down the road with a bag of kitchen waste on the back of my bike, but it's worth it for the end result – barrow-loads of fresh compost that I can dig back into the soil to produce bumper crops of vegetables. But how exactly does compost improve the performance of the vegetables I grow?

In its simplest terms, compost is a rich mix of organic matter – kitchen waste, plant remains, grass clippings and animal manure – piled together so that it rots down to a fine, crumbly consistency. Full of goodness, it is nature's best soil conditioner, replacing the nutrients that have been lost through cultivation, helping to provide plants with what they need to thrive, and improving the structure and texture of the soil. Nothing out of the ordinary, you might think, but, as you'll see, compost is more than just an important addition to the soil – it is absolutely crucial, especially where the ground is cultivated intensively.

The art of decomposition

The process of decomposition itself is hugely complex and involves millions of living organisms working together in a miraculous way. To understand the process on a basic level, imagine a forest floor. Nature creates a yearly cycle of growth and decay: leaves fall in the autumn and mix with other dead vegetation and animal waste in a thick layer, gradually decomposing over a period of months and years. Full of locked–up nutrients in its unrotted state, the matter is broken down by the myriad insects, fungi and bacteria (sometimes known as decomposers) that live in the soil, and is eventually transformed into a brown, crumbly material that is worked down into the earth. During this process, the beneficial nutrients are released, effectively recycled, for plants to use again. This is nature's compost, sometimes known as humus, a general term for decomposed organic matter, and without it, the soil would be starved and unable to support any vegetation at all.

Making compost is man's way of imitating this natural process, although in a vastly accelerated form. Just as in nature, the organic matter is piled together and broken down by bacteria, worms and other creatures but, because it is in a more concentrated form, it decomposes much more quickly. And, as explained later (p.66), there are ways to speed up the decomposition process further by creating a kind of 'super-environment' for the decomposers. The advantages gained from the resulting compost are manifold: when used in your garden, it will improve soil structure, soil fertility, aeration and water retention. Plants will get the nutrients they need to grow healthily and strongly, and they will be more resistant to disease. Homemade compost can also be added to potting mediums, so you don't have to buy potting compost, fertilizers and soil improvers.

Decomposition occurs naturally with the seasons, as leaves mix with other dead vegetation and animal matter, forming layers that build up over the years.

Some benefits of compost and composting

- recycles your organic waste
- reduces pressure on landfill sites
- reduces waste disposal rates and taxes
- creates a free soil conditioner
- saves money on other fertilizers
- lessens the need to use chemicals
- reduces the need to use scarce natural resources like peat in gardens
- suppresses plant diseases
- makes more nutrients available to your plants
- improves soil structure

The secret life of soil

Composting starts and ends with the soil. Remember, while we spend hours trying to make the perfect compost heap, the same process is going on naturally beneath the soil, so it is helpful to know a little about the function and composition of soil before setting out to make your own compost.

Soil is an amazing resource. Vital for the production of food, timber and energy crops, capable of storing water and nutrients, as well as acting as a support system for plants, it plays a pivotal role in agriculture and our environment. Pause a minute to think about the pressures we place on it. Intensive agriculture, urbanization, mineral extraction and landfill waste disposal all result in loss of soil structure, soil erosion and contamination. In urban areas, the soil is disappearing beneath layers of concrete. In the countryside, the use of pesticides and artificial fertilizers in agriculture also takes its toll, while natural erosion and soil depletion occurs through the action of wind and rain. Soil is our life force: surely we should be devising ways to conserve this most precious of resources rather than taking it for granted?

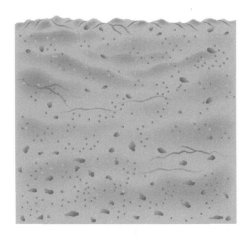

Loam

What is soil?

Soil is made up of four main components: rock or mineral particles, organic matter, air and water. Also present within this structure are millions of living organisms whose function it is to break down the organic matter. Of the solid matter, the rock and mineral content makes up about 90 percent of the total and the remaining 10 percent is organic matter. This 10 percent shouldn't be glossed over, because it is the very crux of what we are talking about. Organic matter, or humus, is what makes soil work. It is impossible to overstate the importance of humus. Without it, a soil will deteriorate, and an unhealthy soil means unhealthy plants. This is why we make compost.

Let's look at the rock and mineral content of the soil. Influenced by many factors including climate, native vegetation and the underlying rock type, each soil has its own texture, determined by the balance of the three main mineral components – sand, clay and silt. All types of soil have these in varying proportions, and they affect the soil's ability to retain water, nutrients and air. Any extreme is undesirable.

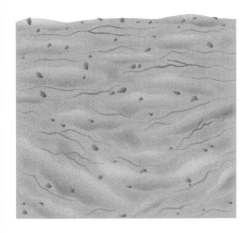

Sand

In an excessively sandy soil, for example, where the soil particles are large, water is liable to flood straight through rather than being stored. Nutrients are washed away too, instead of being made available to the plants. In a clay soil, on the other hand, the soil particles are very small, so they crowd together and tend to exclude air and water. A good balanced and fertile soil with equal parts of silt, sand and clay is the ideal: it is sometimes known as loam. In a loamy soil, the sand, silt and clay particles are grouped together with humus to form larger particles called aggregates. A soil like this is often said to have good 'crumb' structure.

Clay

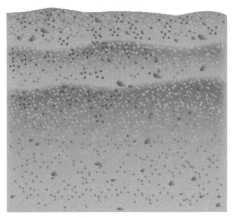

Testing your soil

If you are unsure what kind of soil you have, this simple test might help. Take a large jam jar and half fill it with water. Then fill the jar up to the top with soil, screw the lid on tight and shake it up and down, tipping it upside down to make sure the soil gets well mixed in. Leave the concoction for a day or so and then have a look. The soil will have settled at the bottom of the jar in separate layers, and it should be possible to see the proportions of each main mineral component – ie sand, silt or clay. Sand is the heaviest, so any sand present will be at the bottom of the jar. Silt will form the next layer, with clay particles (the smallest) at the top. Another way to test the soil is simply by feel. Take a handful of soil and squeeze a small amount between your thumb and fingers. If there is a lot of sand, it will feel gritty and it will be crumbly in your hand. If it leaves a smeary mark on your fingers, it contains particles of silt or clay. If it feels sticky and you can roll it into a ball, there is a high proportion of clay.

What is humus?

Now back to that crucial 10 percent organic content. This is what helps plants grow – but it's not as simple as all that. Before nutrients can be made available to the plants, the organic matter has to undergo a complex process of decomposition, carried out by living organisms within the soil.

A healthy soil – one that is not damaged by inappropriate chemicals – is teeming with different forms of life, from earthworms and beetles to the tiniest microorganisms (bacteria, protozoa and fungi). These 'decomposers' break down the organic matter that naturally accumulates on the soil surface and this action makes the nutrients available to plants. The larger organisms like worms, snails and other gastropods, tackle the raw material at surface level, breaking it up and dragging it down below. Earthworms in particular are crucial to this first stage of decomposition, chomping determinedly through soil and organic matter, grinding it down in their gizzards and passing it out the other end as worm casts (a concentrated form of humus that is full of nutrients). In fact the more worms there are the better – they are a good indicator of a balanced healthy soil. I get worried if I don't see any when I'm digging over a bed in my vegetable garden. However, the unsung heroes are the millions of microorganisms that continue the work under the soil surface – and there are phenomenal armies of them (up to 600 million bacteria in a single gram of earth). Their job is to digest the organic matter, further breaking it down, refining it and converting its chemical components into a form that can easily be taken up by plants. Think about it. Plants don't have digestive systems like humans. They can only use nutrients when they are in a liquid or gaseous state, so they need other organisms to break these substances down for them. When there is plenty of organic matter in the soil, the microorganisms feed on it and multiply, breaking it down into humus and releasing nutrients in the process.

A humus-rich soil will supply most of the elements plants need to survive – not in huge quantities, but enough to provide a good start. The main nutrients that plants require for growth are nitrogen (N), phosphorus (P) and potassium (K): these are sometimes known as macronutrients. Nitrogen is essential to the formation of plant tissue, particularly stems and leaves, and the demand for it is especially high when the plant is young and growth is most rapid. Signs of a nitrogen deficiency are stunted growth of a sickly pale yellowy green colour. Phosphorus is essential for photosynthesis and for the development of flowers and fruit – it is more necessary as the plant matures than in the early stages of growth. A plant suffering from phosphorus deficiency will have reddish or purple discoloration on the undersides of the leaves. Potassium is used most notably for root development, and it helps the plant retain water. Signs of deficiency include brown leaf edges that may later crinkle or curl. Humus also helps to supply a whole host of lesser elements, known as micronutrients, that plants also need for healthy growth. These include copper, iron, zinc, iodine and cobalt, as well as carbon dioxide, which is released into the atmosphere as the soil organisms break down the carbon element of the organic matter.

In praise of humus

One of the advantages of humus (and therefore also of compost) over artificial products is that it has a kind of slow-release mechanism, which means that the nutrients are supplied to the plants over a long period of time. Some chemical compounds are made available to plants in the first few months of being in the soil, but because certain matter takes longer to break down (for example, cellulose or lignin, the woody substance in the walls of plant cells), others are released over a period of about two years. And – this is even more ingenious – the nutrients are made available when the plants need them most, because the activity of the soil organisms increases when the soil warms up in spring, which is when plants are growing quickest and require most food. Most artificial fertilizers, on the other hand, are quick-fixers that benefit your plants only in the short term. They may even saturate the plant with too many nutrients at once, resulting in excess chemicals leaching away with the rain. In the case of nitrogen fertilizers, this is a very real problem, causing nitrate pollution in surface water and rivers.

Consisting mainly of rotted organic matter, humus also contains the cells and skeletons of all the microorganisms that have taken part in the decomposition process. Because of this bulk, it is excellent for improving soil structure, no matter what kind of soil you have. Humus literally binds the soil particles to form aggregates (larger particles). This is assisted by the action of the soil microorganisms which, when they are forming humus, produce sticky secretions that help to hold everything together. In sandy soil, humus improves the structure by filling the gaps between the large particles and therefore helping water retention. In clay soil, it clings to the smaller particles, making them bigger and allowing more air into the soil.

Another major advantage of humus is that it improves the

aeration of a soil – and oxygen, of course, is essential to the life of the soil organisms. One of the most noticeable signs of a poorly aerated soil is a crust, known as a hard pan, developing on the surface. Because aggregates aren't forming, the soil becomes compacted, and the resultant hard pan limits the entry of air (and water) into it. Seeds will fare particularly badly in these conditions, finding it difficult to break through the compaction. The soil will also be more susceptible to erosion by wind and rain. In general terms, the more humus there is, the better aerated the soil is, the less compacted it becomes and the more efficiently it drains. It will also be able to hold water more efficiently, and therefore have an improved ability to hold on to nutrients. A healthy soil should have a reasonably high percentage of both air and water – about 25 percent each – in order for the soil organisms to perform at optimum levels; adding humus in the form of compost will help maintain this balance.

Yet another plus point for humus is the fact that it can help to prevent disease spreading into plants, as Sir Albert Howard first discovered in the early twentieth century (see p.10). The reason for this is that humus supports millions of microorganisms. Some of these are bacteria that cause disease, but if the soil life is diverse enough, the baddies can be cancelled out by the beneficial organisms. In addition to this, humus promotes the growth of other organisms that contain natural antibiotics, further strengthening the plants against disease.

Whichever way you look at it, humus is doing nothing but good – it even helps to warm the soil up in spring, its dark colour absorbing the heat. Add these to the benefits of making your own compost and you have a winning formula: you're recycling your organic waste, creating a free soil conditioner, making your plants more resistant to disease, and supplying them with the nutrients they need when they need them. It's not difficult to see why those who are already committed organic gardeners regard compost as the backbone of the garden.

The benefits of humus in a soil

- acts as a slow-release fertilizer, supplying the main nutrients that a plant needs over a long period of time

- helps to form aggregates by the action of soil microorganisms that release sticky secretions to hold soil particles together

- improves soil structure because of its bulky composition

- helps water and nutrient retention because of its porous, spongy nature

- ensures sufficient aeration in soil

- provides good drainage

- helps prevent wind and water erosion

- supports a wide range of soil bacteria, including those that produce natural antibiotics to fight against plant disease

- moderates soil temperature

The science of composting

When I first started making compost, I read up on the basics and learnt the practicalities, but it wasn't until I found out about how it all worked that I began to get the best results. Remember that in making compost you're acting as a facilitator rather than a creator. You're setting up the right conditions for a whole host of creatures to do the work for you, and until you know exactly how they work and what they need, you'll be shooting in the dark. It's like playing a sport without knowing all the rules and skills that are involved – once you know everything there is to know, you're in a much better position to improve. In the same way, it is helpful to know exactly what is going on in your heap, so that you can achieve the optimum conditions for decomposition.

Like the soil itself, a compost heap contains a wide diversity of living things. In fact, an active heap has more life in it than the soil because of the concentration of all the elements that the various microorganisms, or bacteria, need to thrive. Soil microorganisms are the main catalysts in the heap, breaking down the raw material into simpler forms of carbohydrates and proteins through enzymatic digestion. The carbohydrates then break down into simple sugars, organic acids and carbon dioxide, while the proteins are transformed into peptides, amino acids, ammonium compounds, atmospheric nitrogen and, finally, nitrate, which is the form of nitrogen that is available to plants. Along with all other living things, bacteria need sufficient moisture and oxygen to survive and thrive, as well as the right amounts of carbon and nitrogen. If conditions are favourable in the compost heap, they can multiply at an amazing rate, reproducing by binary fission (literally splitting in two) every five or six minutes or so. Ensuring the bacteria get what they need is the key to good composting.

Like the soil itself, a compost heap contains a wide diversity of living things. In fact, an active heap has more life in it than the soil because of the concentration of all the elements that the various microorganisms, or bacteria, need to thrive.

Carbon and nitrogen

Bacteria use carbon for energy and nitrogen to grow and reproduce. They get energy from oxidizing the carbon (turning it into carbon dioxide) – and the heat in a compost heap is the result of this oxidization, as they 'burn' up the carbon. Getting the right balance between carbon and nitrogen is crucial: if the bacteria have too much or too little of either of these elements they will die. It might help to think 'brown' and 'green' when trying to identify the sources of these two elements – the carbon-rich sources, such as straw, leaves and woody matter, are brown, while the sources high in nitrogen are green – fresh grass clippings and kitchen waste, for example. The main component of the organic matter should be carbon, with just enough nitrogen to help the decomposition: about 30 parts carbon to 1 part nitrogen. All plants contain both carbon and nitrogen, so this ratio is based on the amounts of carbon and nitrogen in each plant, not simply the volume of green and brown materials – if you made your compost with 30 times as much brown material, it would take years to rot down! So, for example, dead leaves have a C/N ratio of approximately 40:1, while fresh grass clippings are 20:1. If they are mixed together, the C/N ratio averages out at 30:1. Therefore, roughly speaking, you should mix half green and half brown to end up with the right formula. There is more on the balance of materials later (p.35/ch4).

Air and water

Air and water are the other elements that the bacteria need to thrive. As the process of decomposition takes place, any oxygen in the heap is used up. The decomposition becomes anaerobic and microbial life will start to die off. To get it going again, and to ensure that you get your finished compost sooner, the oxygen needs to be replaced; this is done by turning the heap with a fork or an aerator (a special tool made for this purpose). Water is just as important as oxygen. The ideal is to have the moisture content in the heap at about 50 percent. If it falls below 40 percent the activity of the micro-organisms will start to slow down, if it exceeds 60 percent, it will filter into air spaces, thereby pushing down the oxygen content.

How decomposition takes place

Now we get to the real nitty gritty. This is the point that we take a magnifying glass – or a microscope to be precise – to the heap to spy on the millions of creatures that make our compost for us. Let's start from the moment you throw your first scraps on the pile.

Almost immediately, the bacteria get to work. The first to arrive on the scene are the psychrophiles, bacteria that survive in low temperatures of around 13°C (55°F). As they digest the carbon compounds, they start to alter the chemical state of the organic matter, giving off small amounts of energy that eventually raise the temperature of the pile enough for the next group of bacteria. These are the mesophiles, mid-temperature bacteria that thrive at about 20–30°C (68–86°F). Most of the decomposition that takes place in a compost heap is mesophilic and this group of bacteria are extremely efficient decomposers, so if your pile doesn't reach higher temperatures, it doesn't matter, as decomposition will still take place at an adequate rate. During this mid-temperature phase, larger creatures like worms and insects are working in tandem with the mesophiles, breaking the material down into smaller pieces by eating and digesting it – if the matter has been shredded beforehand, more surface area is exposed to the bacteria, which will speed things up.

Provided that the conditions are exactly right (ie the carbon/nitrogen ratio is well balanced, there is enough air and water, and the pile is big enough), the temperature will rise further, paving the way for the thermophiles, which need temperatures of 40–70°C (104–158°F) to survive. Decomposition is now in full swing, and the heat can get so intense that it is possible to boil eggs in the middle of the heap! The thermophiles can only sustain this temperature for three to five days before dying back, however, if the heap is turned after this stage, to provide a new fix of air, the cycle can happen again. In fact, it can happen up to three or four times, if the material isn't already fully decomposed. Thermophilic temperatures are only reached in compost heaps that are carefully managed, with the right balance of materials added in large quantities, but the advantage of such a hot heap is that weed seeds and diseases will be destroyed. Once the heat drops, microbial activity starts to decrease, and other organisms take over to complete the rotting process. At these mid-temperatures, fungi such as actinomycetes and streptomycetes are at

Provided conditions are right, the temperature of a compost heap can rise as high as 70°C (158°F).

work, producing natural antibiotics that keep disease at bay. You know these organisms are present when you see white, cobwebby structures – a sign of good, healthy compost. Other organisms include nematodes and protozoa, mites and wolf spiders, centipedes and ground beetles and, of course, the invaluable worm. You may see great tangles of worms in the heap at this stage. These aren't the usual big earthworms that you see when you're digging the soil, but smaller varieties known as red worms, brandling worms or tiger worms (*Eisenia foetida*). Don't be squeamish; just remember how much good they're doing and learn to love them. You may also find slugs and snails – again, there is no harm in this because they too are helping to break the matter down. The only trouble with letting them join the feast is that when the compost runs out they'll look elsewhere for their food.

Once the worms start to disappear, you know that the compost is almost done. If the conditions are perfect and the temperatures are high enough, a batch of compost can be

Worms are essential in the decomposition process. Those found in the compost heap aren't common earthworms (above) but smaller varieties known as red worms, tiger worms or brandling worms (right).

ready in less than six weeks; it is much more likely, however, to take months rather than weeks for a heap to rot down fully, since most people don't have the time or volume of material to get temperatures up to thermophilic levels, which is when decomposition rates are fastest. In a perfect world, when fully decomposed, the compost should be transformed into a fine dark brown mixture with the appearance of good crumbly chocolate cake, smelling of nothing but clean earth. In reality, though, most people's compost doesn't look like the stuff made by the experts on TV gardening programmes. Don't worry. It can always be sieved, and anyway, a bit of roughness in the texture can help the soil structure.

> Be wary of using the fresh compost too quickly: it's better to leave it for several more weeks until you're sure the microbial life has died down completely. This is because the compost will use up valuable nitrogen in the soil if it is still decomposing, rather than giving it back for the plants to use.

Be wary of using the fresh compost too quickly: it's better to leave it for several more weeks until you're sure the microbial life has died down completely. This is because the compost will use up valuable nitrogen in the soil if it is still decomposing, rather than giving it back for the plants to use.

Isn't nature astounding? From the minute you pile your material together, complex chains of bacteria are working at a frenzied pace, quickly accelerating to a crescendo of activity, and then dying down to be taken over by other forms of life. If you're an impatient or disillusioned composter, take some time to understand the process, and you'll be in a much better position to produce compost that will be the envy of your gardening neighbours. After all, it works both ways. When you're giving the bacteria and other organisms what they need, they'll reward you by working more efficiently. If you were managing a big company, wouldn't you want to get the best out of your employees by making them happy? It's the same principle.

Organisms at work in a compost heap

- psychrophiles: lower temperature bacteria that start off the decomposition process

- mesophiles: mid-temperature bacteria that thrive at temperatures of 20–30°C (68–86°F)

- thermophiles: the heat-lovers, working at temperatures of 40–70°C (104–158°F)

- fungi, such as actinomycetes and streptomycetes, that produce natural antibiotics

- nematodes: invertebrates that prey upon bacteria, protozoa and fungal spores

- mites, feeding on the yeasts that are in fermenting material

- springtails, whose main food source is fungi

- wolf spiders, which build no webs but run around freely, preying on arthropods

- centipedes, found frequently in soil communities

- ground beetles, feeding on other organisms, seeds and vegetable matter

- slugs and snails, which help to break down the organic matter

- red worms or tiger worms, which consume organic matter and pass it as worm casts

Composing compost

Making compost is like cooking. If you have the right ingredients, in the right proportions, you'll end up with satisfactory results. And the key to the right ingredients, as we've seen, is to provide the decomposers (bacteria and other organisms) with the conditions they need, most importantly the correct balance between carbon and nitrogen. The ideal ratio is 30 parts carbon to 1 part nitrogen, which equals about half carbon-rich and half nitrogen-rich materials. Diversity is also important – a compost made with a good mix of materials will contain a wider variety of nutrients and micronutrients, and if the contents are very diverse, it is more likely that these elements will be returned to the plants. In addition, a larger proliferation of beneficial bacteria will be present to counteract disease pathogens.

The joy of composting is that you use the materials you have to hand – from kitchen scraps to plant waste – with a few extras sourced from elsewhere if necessary. The basic rule is that anything that was once part of a plant or animal can be used in the mix, but within these parameters, there are a few dos and don'ts that should be observed. Meat and dairy scraps can be composted, but it is generally recommended that they aren't used in small-scale piles as special conditions are needed for them to decompose safely. They will also attract vermin and flies and smell awful as they rot down. Dog, cat and human faeces should be avoided as they can contain parasites and diseases that can be transferred back into humans via plants. Cat faeces is especially dangerous because it may contain the parasite *Toxoplasma gondii*, which has been known to cause infant blindness.

Farm animal manure isn't an essential ingredient of the compost heap, but it certainly helps, both as a valuable source of nitrogen, and also because it contains large numbers of bacteria, which will aid rapid decomposition. Horse and cattle manure are often available free from stables and farms. Chicken manure is also valuable and contains the highest levels of nitrogen, phosphorus and potassium. Other less frequently used manures that can be added to your compost, if you feel so inclined, are duck or goose droppings, rabbit pellets, goat dung and even bat guano! City dwellers without ready supplies of manure needn't worry – there are plenty of other ingredients that are high in nitrogen (see the list of what to add to your heap). However, if you're determined, search around for a 'city' farm, there is a surprising number of them, even in inner-city areas (see useful addresses, p.119).

Composting notes

- Plant material forms the main bulk of any compost heap, but when you're starting your pile, think broadly and you'll find that there are plenty of other things that fall under the umbrella of 'organic matter'

- Don't get too hung up about not having all the right ingredients. If you can't find enough in your own kitchen and back garden, consider asking a non-gardening neighbour to save their kitchen waste for you or finish up a walk in the woods by collecting a few dustbin bags of leaves

- There are no hard and fast rules about exactly what to compost – some people swear by a formula of two parts plant waste to one part manure, others just use grass clippings and leaves – simply aim to get an even balance between greens and browns, and you'll be well on the way to making good compost

What to add to your heap

Nitrogen-rich green materials

Kitchen scraps

Keep a bucket with a lid in your kitchen to collect all your kitchen scraps as you cook. The materials listed tend to be soft and moist, and need to be mixed with drier things to allow air circulation. On their own, kitchen scraps decompose anaerobically and can start to smell unpleasant, so make sure they don't hang around in your kitchen for too long.

- Potato peelings and other vegetable peelings
  - Apple cores
  - Coffee grounds
  - Tea bags
  - Crushed eggshells (a rich source of calcium)
  - Stale bread and cakes

Make sure your compost is protected from scavenging animals.

Save all your fruit and vegetable scraps in a bucket, and add them to the compost heap as often as you can.

Other household waste

Surprisingly, the contents of a vacuum cleaner make a good ingredient. You may think this is just dust, but actually it consists of tiny particles of soil and other organic matter and is high in nitrogen. You can even use hair from a hair brush (human, dog or cat).

Grass

Grass clippings are reasonably high in nitrogen, and if you have a large lawn they may be one of the most plentiful sources of organic matter for composting. Don't put them on in a thick layer, however, because they will mat together to form a smelly, slimy mess, which will exclude air from the pile. Mix them with woody brown materials, like straw or leaves. Avoid using grass that has been sprayed with chemical pesticides or herbicides.

Weeds

Most young weeds can be added to the compost heap and are a valuable source of nitrogen. It is, however, best to avoid pernicious weeds like bindweed and couch grass, and also large weeds with tap roots. If the weeds have gone to seed, only add them if you know your compost is going to reach a temperature high enough to kill them off. If you have a cool heap, be wary of adding any weeds at all.

Animal manure

Regularly adding small amounts of poultry, horse or cattle manure to your compost heap will help decomposition. Manure is very high in nitrogen and it can literally burn plants if used when fresh, so it is essential to make sure that it is well rotted before digging it into your garden. When you add it to the compost heap, make sure that it is mixed with plenty of carbon-rich material to balance its high nitrogen content. Horse manure tends to contain weed seeds, but mixing it with straw will help to get the temperatures up to kill these.

Soft prunings

Anyone who has a garden will have plants to prune from time to time, and soft prunings – from a privet hedge, for example – can be added to the compost heap.

Seaweed

If you live near the sea, a little seaweed can help the compost heap enormously, as it is an excellent source of trace elements.

Comfrey and nettles

Both these plants grow like wildfire and are extremely high in nitrogen. If you can obtain large quantities, they can be torn up and added in a layer, acting as activators in the heap (see p.66).

Feathers

Feathers are surprisingly high in nitrogen, so if you have been plucking poultry, save the feathers to add to the compost heap.

Carbon-rich brown materials

Newspaper, paper and cardboard

Crumpled newspaper and shredded cardboard are under-rated ingredients of the compost heap. If you have a high percentage of wet, nitrogen-rich kitchen waste, it can be extremely valuable to add them to the heap (crumpling allows air circulation). Cereal packets and loo rolls can be used, as well as tissues and unbleached paper. Don't add bleached paper as it contains chlorine, which can be harmful to the living organisms in the heap. (Newspaper is safe because the ink used is biodegradable.) It's probably best to avoid glossy magazines and fruit juice cartons that are lined with plastic or foil.

Dead leaves

Brown leaves are a good source of carbon, but like grass clippings, they can mat together and exclude air, so make sure they are mixed well with other ingredients. Some leaves, such as plane and chestnut, take years to rot down, so avoid these. Steer clear of evergreen leaves like holly and laurel, too. Some people prefer to compost their leaves separately to make leafmould (see p.98).

Straw

Straw has few nutrients, but its thick stems allow air to penetrate the compost pile, so it is beneficial. It needs to be moistened, otherwise it will take an age to rot down.

Old plant remains

If you have a large garden you will probably generate large quantities of plant waste, especially if you grow vegetables. Older plants are woodier and less nitrogen-rich than young plants, and are a good source of bulk for the heap. They should be shredded or chopped into 15–25cm (6–10in) lengths before adding to the compost. You can also use spent cut flowers. Don't add diseased plants; they could re-infect the garden when the compost is used the following year. Diseased plant material should be burnt.

Tree prunings, sticks and twigs

Every compost heap needs a certain proportion of dry, twiggy material to balance the soft, wet stuff. Old brambles, evergreen prunings and other shrubby material can all be used, but must be shredded first. If you have large quantities of such plants, consider buying a mechanical shredder (see p.91). When shredded, this material is also useful as a mulch.

Wood chips, bark and sawdust

Wood products are low in nitrogen, and take a long time to break down, so should only be used if your compost heap is generating enough heat. Coarse wood chips are best avoided as they take a long time to rot down, but can be used in very small quantities. Sawdust should be mixed evenly into the heap or used in very thin layers. Don't use wood that has been chemically treated, as it could add toxins to your compost.

Wood ash

Small amounts of wood ash can be good for a compost heap, because it is high in potash (potassium carbonate). Sprinkle it on in very thin layers only. Don't use coal ash or charcoal ash, however. Coal ash contains large quantities of sulphur and iron, both of which can be toxic to plants, while charcoal takes hundreds or even thousands of years to rot down!

Do not compost

- cat and dog faeces
- human faeces
- meat, bones and fatty food wastes
- dairy products
- pernicious weeds such as bindweed
- diseased plants
- chemically-treated wood products
- coal or charcoal ash

Compost recipes

For an average household with a small garden

This recipe gives you an idea of the kind of ingredients that will make a good, balanced compost. The amounts are based on an average household's weekly kitchen and garden waste. The moist, nitrogen-rich kitchen waste is balanced by shredded leaves and a little cardboard and newspaper.

4 banana skins
14 used teabags
4 cups coffee grounds
5 apple cores
4 quarters melon skin

6 mouldy tomatoes
1 large bowl of potato or vegetable peelings
1 egg carton, shredded
Several sheets of newspaper, crumpled
1 old pot plant, with soil
1 bucket of leaves, shredded

Mix all ingredients together thoroughly and place them in the composting container. Add more material as it becomes available, until the container is filled to the brim. Cover and leave for a week or so before turning.

For the owners of a large garden

This recipe is based on the amount of plant waste generated by a larger garden or allotment. The large amounts of twiggy, carbon-rich material are balanced by the moist kitchen waste and the partially rotted horse manure.

1 bucket moist kitchen waste
$1/2$ bucket semi-rotted horse manure mixed with straw
1 wheelbarrow of spent runner bean plants, shredded
1 wheelbarrow of spent marigold plants, shredded
1 bag of hedge clippings, shredded

Mix all the ingredients as above.

Compost bins

Using a bin or container of some kind for your compost isn't strictly necessary, but it helps to keep it neat and tidy, protects it from wind and rain, prevents unwanted animals from getting in and helps to retain heat and moisture – so, in general terms, a bin produces compost more speedily than a pile on the ground.

When it comes to deciding what kind of container to use, be realistic. If you have a garden the size of a pocket handkerchief and you don't generate vast amounts of green waste, there's no point in having a large compost bin. This is the sort of situation where it may be best not to have any sort of container at all, and just pile your waste in a heap. If, on the other hand, you have acres of land and a productive vegetable garden, you'll need something with more capacity – perhaps a three-bin system (see p.52). Whatever your set-up, there is plenty of choice out there. If you're inventive, it's very easy to make your own, using whatever materials you have to hand: old doors and window frames, random bits of fencing, wooden boxes, hay bales, heavy duty plastic bags, dustbins.

Making compost is all about recycling, after all. In addition, there are hundreds of different composters for sale from garden centres or catalogues, and they are sometimes even sold cheaply by local authorities.

Plastic containers are available in all shapes and sizes from garden centres.

Design tips

Whatever type of container you choose, the foundation is important. Ideally, the bin should be raised slightly off the ground, with a base that allows air to circulate from below (wooden slats or chicken wire, for example). My box-shaped composter has a tough plastic mesh at the bottom and is raised up on five bricks (four round the outside and one in the middle). The bin should also be set above bare soil, so that the microorganisms from the soil have direct access into the heap, therefore speeding up the process. This is why compost heaps should not be built on concrete slabs – they may look neater, but they will lack aeration and the soil microbes won't find their way easily into the waste. Aeration from the sides is also important – holes or slats in the sides of the bin will allow air circulation throughout.

A note on wood. Wooden containers have advantages and disadvantages. Wood is often the material that people prefer aesthetically in their garden, but it isn't the longest-lasting: it's a natural material, so when it comes into contact with the compost, it will start to rot. However, the type of wood you choose will lengthen or shorten the time your bin takes to disintegrate. Untreated pine, for example, which is the cheapest form of timber, will rot down most quickly, maybe within three or four years. Untreated hardwoods, such as cedar, are much more expensive, but have natural preservatives so may last eight or ten years. Pressure-treated timber that is designed for outdoor use is probably the best bet. However, the pressure treatment includes chemicals such as copper, chromium and arsenic, so you might be concerned about it coming into contact with your organic compost. The danger of contamination is probably minimal, but to be safe, leave such wood outside to weather for three months before using it. Doing this will allow gases from the chemical compounds to disperse before the compost comes into contact with it. Creosoted wood should be avoided altogether.

A question to ask yourself when deciding on compost bins is: 'Will I be able to get to it easily?' It's all very well having giant boxes with high sides, but are you going to be able to fork the mixture out, or turn it, without climbing a ladder? Many compost systems have removable or hinged fronts, allowing easy access for both turning and removing the finished compost.

Finally, lids. Should the compost be covered or not? I always cover mine, simply because of the amount of rain that would otherwise fall on it: too much water can unbalance the moisture content of the compost heap, and it can also wash valuable nutrients down into the soil below. Another advantage of covering it is that this keeps in the heat. It can be covered with a sheet of plastic, a dustbin liner, tarpaulin or carpet. Keep lighter covers in place with bricks.

Siting your heap

Choosing a site for your compost heap may sound like common sense but there are a few things to bear in mind. For aesthetic reasons, it should probably be located in a discreet corner of the garden, perhaps screened by some hedging, trellis or a wall to shield it from strong winds, and if you have a large garden, locate it in a position that is nearest to the main source of material (ie near the lawn for grass clippings, or near the vegetable garden for the remains of old plants). Don't butt it right up against a wooden fence or shed, however, because the wood will eventually decay. Equally, it shouldn't be sited under a large tree because large amounts of leaves (high in carbon) will slow the decomposition down. The only other factor to take into consideration is siting it near a water source, which can be helpful in long hot summers.

Some ideas for compost containers

Plastic bin liner

One of the most basic containers for compost, for those who are producing small amounts of material, is a tough plastic dustbin bag, with plenty of holes pierced in it for aeration. Mix a good range of materials before putting them in, tie the top and shake every few weeks to aerate the mixture.

Wooden pallet bin

This is one of the simplest (and cheapest) ideas I've come across. Wooden pallets are easy to come by and their slatted construction makes them ideal for building a well-aerated container. You'll need five pallets – one for the base, and four to make up the sides. The four uprights can be wired or screwed together to make the container, which sits on top of the fifth. To make turning the compost easier, you can add hinges and latches onto one of the pallets to create an opening front.

Wire bins

Another simple compost container can be made cheaply from 16-gauge

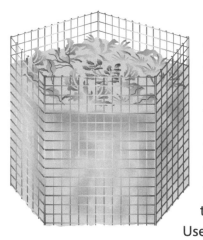

galvanized wire fencing, plastic-coated wire or chicken wire. The most basic bin is a cylinder-shaped enclosure made from a length of wire joined with wire ties. This can easily be moved in order to turn the heap or to harvest the finished compost, simply by undoing the ties and lifting off the wire. Use wire fencing of 1m (3ft) width and before joining it together, bend back 20–30cm (8–12in) at each end to create clean edges with no stray wires sticking out. A more stable version of the cylinder is made by driving four wooden posts into the ground and wrapping the wire around the outside. A five-sided version is even more stable. This time make it with five flat panels of chicken wire, again fastened with wire ties. Where the wire has been cut, bend the stray ends inwards with pliers to create a smooth edge. The bottom wires can be left sticking out to grip the ground. These containers can also be made with plastic-coated wire.

New Zealand box

This is the classic wooden box composter that many of today's designs are based upon. It was first developed by a gardening club in New Zealand, and the design in its simplest form is a wooden structure 1.2m (4ft) square and 1m (3ft) high.

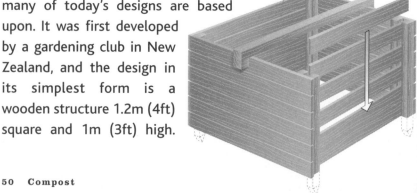

It sits straight on the earth without a bottom, and does not have a lid. The sides consist of wooden slats 15cm (6in) wide by 2.5cm (1in) thick with a 1.5cm ($\frac{1}{2}$in) air space between the boards to help air circulation. The frame is made with 10 by 5cm (4 by 2in) posts. Three sides of boards are screwed onto the frame, while the fourth, the front, is designed so that the individual boards slot down between two posts and can be removed easily when the compost needs turning. There are many variations on this theme, including a square box with four compartments made with removable wooden dividers.

Wooden stackable bin

This design is simple and versatile, and the interlocking sections stacked one on top of another enable you to build up the box as the compost heap increases. As the pile decomposes and begins to get smaller, sections can be taken off one by one and used to start building up another container. You will need to make at least six wooden sections to form a container. Each section is made into a square frame, with four wooden corner blocks that sit on the section below. For step by step instructions on how to build this container, see p.54.

Dustbin

Using an old dustbin for a compost container is an easy solution for those with small gardens and few materials to compost. Get a large plastic dustbin and pierce holes in the bottom, sides and lid using a drill or hammer and nail. Raise the bin on bricks and put a tray underneath to catch any nutritious liquid that may leach out.

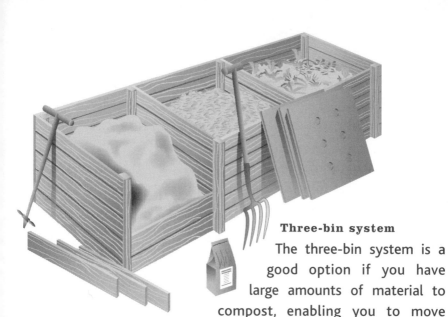

Three-bin system

The three-bin system is a good option if you have large amounts of material to compost, enabling you to move material from one bin to another while turning the heap. It is one of the most efficient ways of composting because it means that you always have one bin for new material, one for partially decomposed material and one for finished compost. A triple version of the wooden New Zealand box described above is a good basis for a design: simply tack on two more boxes to the first. A slight variation on this is to make the second box smaller than the first, and the third smaller again. The first needs to be the biggest because this is where the raw materials go – they have the largest volume and take up the most space. By the time the compost is turned into the second box, after it has been decomposing for a while, it will have shrunk considerably and so needs less space. By the time it is fully decomposed and ready for the third box, it will be less than half its original volume. A decent-sized wooden three-bin system would be 1m (3ft) high, with the width of each box reducing from 1.2m (4ft) to 1m (3ft) to 80cm (32in).

Brick enclosure

Three-sided brick enclosures can be built with or without cement. Building them without cement allows them to be moved if need be. It also means that the bricks can be arranged with a 10–15cm (4–6in) gap between them so that air can circulate easily. Wooden lids and gates can be added if desired.

Rotating barrel

Rotating barrel composters are available commercially, and although they aren't much to look at, they can produce quick results. Materials must be stockpiled before adding in one fell swoop, and the barrel is then turned every few days to mix the material by tipping it from one end to the other.

Methods that don't need containers

Trench composting depends on having enough space to leave parts of the garden free of plants for a few months. Raw compost materials are added to trenches in the garden, covered over, and left to decompose naturally. It can be a slow process, because oxygen is not available; in addition, because nitrogen is needed for the decomposition process, it will take it from the soil, so it's best to wait several months before planting anything in the spot. Some people swear by trench composting for runner beans, but the trench must be dug and filled as early as possible in autumn, so that the compost is well rotted by planting time in spring. Sheet composting is similar to trench composting, but the organic material is spread in a layer on the soil before being tilled in. Again, this means that the soil must be left fallow for a time before being planted, to give the material time to decompose. Finally, there is windrow composting, a variation on the simple compost heap. Windrows are elongated piles that are often used in large-scale municipal composting, and they require large amounts of material to work efficiently.

Making a stackable wooden compost container

You will need:

24 wooden planks, 1m by 150mm (3ft by 6in). The planks can be more or less than 150mm (6in) wide, as long they are all the same width.

24 pieces of batten to form wooden corner blocks 45mm by 45mm by 150mm (1¼in by 1¼in by 6in). If your planks are wider or narrower than 150mm (6in) match the battens to this.

120 40mm (1½in) screws (size no M4)

Building the box

1) Take one of the planks and with a pencil mark three holes 20mm (¾in) in from the end and at equal intervals: the first should be 40mm (1½in) in from the edge of one

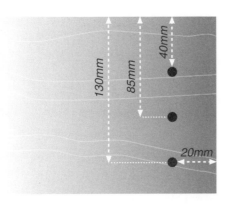

long side of the plank, the second 85mm (3¼in), and the third 130mm (5in). Drill holes clean through each mark. Repeat for the other end of the plank.

2) Place one of the corner blocks under the edge of the plank so that it protrudes by 20mm (¾in) and is flush with the end of the plank, as shown. Set your drill so you can drill the depth of the plank and 30mm (1¼in) into each corner block. Clamp the two together to hold them while drilling. Drill three holes in the corner block, using those in the plank as a guide. Once drilled, fasten the corner block to the plank with three screws. Repeat on the other end of the plank.

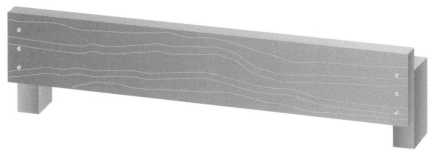

3) Repeat the whole process above with another length of plank.

4) Pre-drill two holes in a third plank, 20mm (¾in) in from the end of the plank and 60mm (2½in) and 105mm (4¼in) from one long edge. Repeat at the other end. Repeat this process on

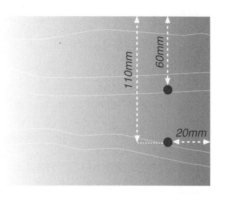

110mm 60mm 20mm

a fourth plank. The third and fourth planks do not have corner blocks.

5) Stand the two planks with corner blocks on end about a metre apart, as shown, and then place the third plank on top. Make sure that the ends of the third plank are flush with the outer edges of the planks with the corner blocks. Set the drill so it can drill the depth of the plank and 30mm (1¼in) into the corner block. Use two screws to fasten the boards together (you may need help to hold everything together while doing this). Repeat at the other end of the plank.

6) Turn the section over and repeat the process with the fourth plank and you will end up with a square frame. Repeat the entire process with the remaining planks and you should end up with six frames that can be stacked as shown.

The art of composting

Now that we've looked at the basics of composting – the process of decomposition and the materials to use – it's time to look at the specifics. How do you go about creating a heap that's going to work for you? Since time began, people have used different methods to make compost. In recent times, some of these methods have been recorded and they can be used as models for our own composting. While some people are content to leave the heap for as long as it takes for nature to take its course, others are anxious to produce as much compost as possible to feed the soil and benefit their plants. Building a compost heap can be as effortless or as time-consuming as you want it to be; however you decide to play it, you'll end up with usable compost – the only difference is the time it takes to produce.

Remember, there is no secret formula, no right or wrong way to make compost. Methods of composting are frequently the topic of heated discussion – everyone has their own idea of what materials to use, how to build the heap, and how often to turn it – but the truth is, as long as you follow a few basic principles, you achieve the same end result.

The Indore method

Sir Albert Howard first developed this method in the 1920s at Indore in India (see p.10). His principles of layering and aerating are still applicable, and are particularly suitable for someone who generates lots of plant waste, such as those with a large garden or allotment.

The materials Howard used were animal manures, brush (twiggy material), straw or hay, leaves and soil, arranged in alternating layers in a wooden bin to a height of 1.5m (5ft). A layer of brush came first, followed by 15cm (6in) of plant matter, 5cm (2in) of manure and then a sprinkling of soil. Howard recommended three parts of plant matter to one part manure. Care was taken to moisten the pile with water while building, and the pile was turned, once after six weeks, and again after 12 weeks. Later, Howard experimented with using human urine and faeces mixed with kitchen waste and materials high in carbon such as straw and leaves. The Indore system is labour-intensive, and the heap doesn't reach extremely high temperatures. It does, however, produce good quality compost in a reasonable length of time.

Cool heap

The easiest method of composting is known as 'passive' or

'cool heap' composting. All you have to do is to pile organic matter in a heap as and when it becomes available, and leave it to its own devices. You don't even have to worry much about the balance of materials with this method, as long as you are aware that decomposition could take a very long time – from six months to two years, depending on the raw materials that go into it. If you only need small amounts of compost, and have a busy life, this is the method for you.

Hot heap

The 'active' or 'hot heap' is the method to use if you want to produce compost quickly. You can't afford to hang around when you're cultivating a patch of land intensively – the more plants you grow, the faster you need to replace the goodness that they take out. Like a hungry child, the soil needs feeding regularly, and the quicker you can come up with the goods the better. In order to achieve this, you need to devote time to building and tending the heap, and thinking about its contents. In active or hot heap composting, you have to manage the heap carefully and this results in the temperature being raised higher by the activity of millions of bacteria, thereby speeding up the decomposition process.

The CAT high-fibre method

However, compost heaps don't necessarily have to reach furnace-like temperatures to succeed (p.29). Compost that has reached only mesophilic (medium) temperatures is produced almost as efficiently. Moreover, research has shown that finished compost from a hot temperature heap sometimes lacks the beneficial antibiotic-producing soil organisms that are present in lower temperature heaps, because it gets too hot for them to survive. Today, many people are swinging away from the textbook hot heap composting method in favour of a more laid–back approach.

In the 1990s, the members of the Centre for Alternative Technology in Wales began researching a 'new' method of composting. Ideal for small-scale composting, their 'high-fibre' system is based on the principle of mixing kitchen waste with waste paper and cardboard. You don't need large amounts of material, and because the compost is made from purely household rubbish, you don't need a garden to be able to make it! The paper and cardboard is carbon-rich, forming an ideal foil for the nitrogen-rich kitchen waste, mopping up excess moisture, keeping the heap well ventilated and breaking down rapidly. Materials such as used tissues, cereal boxes and egg cartons can all be used, torn or crumpled first to create more air spaces. Newspaper can also be put on this sort of heap, although CAT recommends the normal recycling route for it, simply because most households have so much. (Printing inks do not contain heavy metals, so are perfectly safe in your compost.)

Building and maintaining the heap

In the high-fibre system a layer of crumpled cardboard and paper is put in the bottom of a container, ideally with some worm-rich compost from a previous batch or from someone else's compost bin. Then the soft kitchen waste is fed into the container as it arises, mixed with more paper and cardboard. Other 'soft' nitrogen-rich waste from the garden can be used as well.

This is not a fast method of composting – it can take up to a year to harvest the first batch of compost – but it is a highly effective way to recycle ordinary household waste and involves very little maintenance. Once established, the heap needs minimal attention, other than adding material as it becomes available. It does not reach high temperatures, but relies more heavily on the larger decomposers like worms to do the work. If decomposition is very slow, it might be necessary to buy a batch of brandling or tiger worms (see chapter 7) to get the heap going.

Heap maintenance

As we've seen, there are advantages and disadvantages with both hot and cool heaps. Most people should be able to find a happy medium, working with the materials they have to hand, and with the time available to them. What I want to do is to show how to produce good quality compost at a reasonable rate, and the key to this is creating the perfect living conditions for the decomposers.

To survive at optimum levels, the bacteria need the right balance of carbon and nitrogen, and enough quantities of air and water, so carbon-rich (brown) and nitrogen-rich (green) materials should be added in roughly equal quantities. A good

Build up layers of nitrogen-rich (green) and carbon-rich (brown) material for optimum results.

general rule is to alternate layers of green and brown materials in layers of about 5–8cm (2–3in), but mixing the materials together thoroughly after adding them to the heap is just as effective. Think about textures, too. If there are too many soft, moist materials, air will be excluded, the decomposition will become anaerobic and the heap will start smelling. This is usually a result of nitrogen being released into the air as ammonia. Use common sense: if you add a large bucketful of moist, nitrogen-rich kitchen waste, balance it by adding an armful of straw or dry leaves. You may think twiggy material will hinder the process by taking longer to rot down, but in fact it is essential to an efficient compost heap because it allows air to circulate during the first stages of decomposition, when the bacteria need it most.

Water

Water and air are key requirements for an efficient compost heap (see p.28, ch3). The moisture content should be 50 percent: the classic yardstick, mentioned in nearly all literature on composting, is that the compost should feel like a well-wrung sponge. But it's virtually impossible to gauge the moisture content exactly, so the main thing is to keep an eye on it – if it looks too dry, sprinkle it with water or insert a hose well into the pile so that it gets wet throughout, if looks too wet, add some dry material like straw, twigs or newspaper. If you're using the layering method, it is always a good idea to sprinkle water on between layers as you build the heap up.

Air

Having a well-aerated heap is necessary if you want to produce good compost in a reasonable time span – like all living things, bacteria need oxygen to survive. This should be considered when building or selecting a container (see above, p.46). Whatever design you go for, make sure that there are gaps or holes to allow air to circulate and that the container is raised up on timber or bricks to allow circulation from the bottom. The other way to add air to the heap is to turn it regularly. This is usually done with a fork – very good for the arm muscles – but if you are less able-bodied buy a rotating barrel composter that mixes the compost with the turn of a handle. Other methods for aerating include inserting hollow pipes into the centre of the heap or at various intervals throughout, and you can even buy special compost aerators with propellor-like wings to twist within the heap.

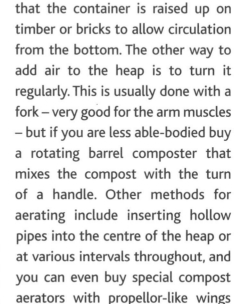

Turning the heap regularly keeps it well aerated - the more oxygen available to the bacteria, the more efficiently they will work.

Turning

There are no hard and fast rules for the frequency of turning your compost heap – indeed you don't have to turn it at all. I find that turning it every three or four weeks is adequate, but if you're really attentive and are determined to get the temperature up, it can be turned every three or four days, preferably just after the initial burst of heat has died down (use a compost thermometer to measure the heat). As the material decomposes, the pile gets smaller, the oxygen gradually runs out and so the decomposing bacteria start dying off and the temperature decreases. This is the optimum time for turning the heap. Material around the edge of the pile that hasn't rotted down as much as that in the centre where the temperatures are hottest, will provide more food for the bacteria, and the injection of air will encourage a repeat of the initial activity, making temperatures rise again.

The size of the heap, whether in a container or on the ground, should be at least 1m (3ft) wide by 1m (3ft) high, which is large enough to retain heat and moisture, but small enough to remain aerated in the centre, as long as it is frequently turned.

Size matters

Bearing all these things in mind, you're well on the way to creating the perfect environment for the compost bacteria, but there are yet more ways to speed up the process. You can help by chopping and shredding the organic waste into smaller pieces. This means that there is more surface area for the bacteria to tackle – more entry points into the material – and they have to do less work in breaking it down into smaller particles. Use garden shears or secateurs to cut everything into pieces 10–15cm (4–6in) long at most.

If you have a large garden and are composting lots of shrubby material or leaves, it might be worth investing in a shredder (see p.93).

The size of your compost heap can also affect the speed of decomposition. A larger pile will generate more heat because its centre will be insulated. The ultimate way to make compost is to collect the different materials – soft, green waste and hard, twiggy brown waste that may need shredding – in separate buckets or bins until you have large amounts of everything, then layer these in a large pile. This can have excellent results, generating the highest temperatures and therefore the quickest decomposition. But, don't worry, most people have busy lives and can only build their compost up as and when the material becomes available. So long as the compost reaches mesophilic temperatures (see p.29), it will decompose perfectly adequately and over a reasonably short period of time. The size of the heap, whether in a container or on the ground, should be at least 1m (3ft) wide by 1m (3ft) high, which is large enough to retain heat and moisture, but small enough to remain aerated in the centre, as long as it is frequently turned.

When to start a heap

You can start a compost heap at any time you want, and once established, the heap can be added to at any time. If you're composting for the first time, however, it might be easier to start building your heap in spring. This is because everything rots down faster through spring and summer – the decomposers need warmth to be active. If you start a heap in the spring, by the summer you'll have built up a good volume of material that should cook down nicely, ready to be used in autumn.

Speeding up your compost

If you're still searching around for ways to speed up the process, you could consider a compost activator. Anything high in nitrogen can work as an activator. Your nose may wrinkle at this, but human urine is one of the best additions for a nitrogen fix: it is entirely sterile, so it can't be harmful, and as well as containing a high percentage of nitrogen, it is also crammed with minerals and vitamins. Many an owner of a vegetable patch (mostly male it has to be said) confesses to having the occasional pee on the compost heap – after dark of course – and it really does work.

Another tip is to add a layer or two of a nitrogen-rich plant to get things going. Comfrey is one of the best. It grows like wildfire once you've established a clump and won't mind in the least being robbed of its leaves every now and again to go into the compost. And, if you've been wondering what to do with that encroaching tangle of nettles at the bottom of the garden, get out your gloves, pull up the nettles, shred them and feed them into your compost, because they are also extremely high in nitrogen.

Finally, an extra dose of manure will never go amiss. Well-rotted manure is best – fresh manure is not as beneficial because it produces frenzied bacterial activity, with the organisms giving out bursts of energy over a very short period before burning themselves out.

Commercial activators are also available from garden centres and mail-order catalogues. These are usually in the form of powders or granules and contain live (but dormant) bacteria and enzymes, similar to those found in soil. Activated by water, they increase the microbial content of the heap. Throwing the occasional spadeful of soil or fresh compost onto the new pile has the same effect, but don't overdo it because it can clog things up.

Tips for success

- Make sure there is a good balance between materials that are high in carbon and those that are high in nitrogen (roughly half green and half brown materials)

- Layer the green and brown materials or mix together thoroughly

- Water as you go: the contents of the heap should be roughly 50 percent water

- Turn the heap frequently to provide enough oxygen for the microorganisms

- Ensure that the volume of the heap is at least 1m (3ft) wide by 1m (3ft) high

- Add high-nitrogen activators such as urine, manure or comfrey

- Add commercial biological activators

Common problems

Many people start composting with enthusiasm, and then give up after a few months because they 'can't get it right'. Here are a few common problems and suggestions for putting them right.

Problem: The compost heap starts to smell unpleasant.

Solution: This is usually because too much moist, nitrogen-rich material (such as kitchen waste) has been added. Balance it by adding dry material such as twigs or straw. It can also be a sign that there isn't enough oxygen, so the pile should be turned.

Problem: The compost heap is too dry.

Solution: This can happen in hot weather and it will slow decomposition down considerably. Insert a hose pipe into the heap and moisten it throughout.

Problem: Nothing seems to be rotting down.

Solution: Be patient! Make sure you have the correct balance of materials, ensure that the compost mixture is neither too wet or too dry, and consider adding a compost activator.

Problem: The heap won't get hot.

Solution: It doesn't matter too much if your compost heap isn't reaching high temperatures. Everything will still decompose at low temperatures, but it will just take longer. To reach high temperatures, add large amounts of material all at once, ensuring that you are getting the right carbon to nitrogen ratio, and turn the heap regularly.

Problem: The finished compost isn't uniformly fine and crumbly.

Solution: Don't worry too much about the appearance of your compost. If you have added lots of twiggy material, there will always be bits that take longer to rot down. If you're really worried about it, sift the compost and return the larger particles to the heap.

Problem: There isn't as much compost as you expected.

Solution: The size of your compost heap can reduce by as much as 60 percent during the decomposition process. Try to anticipate this when calculating how much compost you'll need.

Turning to worms

All the composting methods mentioned so far depend on you having some outside space, but what if you have no garden at all and still want to compost? Don't despair: there is a very good alternative method that can be carried out on a balcony, in a garage or even indoors. Vermicomposting, or worm composting, has become increasingly popular in the last few years and it is by far the best way to compost kitchen waste. Worms are introduced into a box or bin full of high-fibre bedding material. They swiftly eat through this and any kitchen scraps that are added, and what comes out the other end is nutrient-rich casts (droppings).

Worms are so efficient at breaking the material down that they can get through at least their own weight in organic matter every day. Even better, as they digest it, the secretions in their intestinal tracts liberate more plant nutrients, so that the resulting humus contains five times more nitrogen, seven times more phosphorus and 11 times more potassium than normal compost – and there's no doubt about it, plants love the stuff.

Don't be put off by having to handle the worms. I have to confess to battling with an irrational squeamishness before finally deciding to buy a worm bin to sit outside my back door at home. I soon got over that hitch, however, and am now totally converted – once you understand how the worms work, the whole process is completely fascinating. My worm bin recycles most of my kitchen waste, and is used in conjunction with the larger-scale compost heaps on my vegetable patch, which are regularly stocked up with dead plant matter, leaves, manure and grass clippings (and, therefore, don't need kitchen waste on top). The resulting worm compost can be used both in my garden and on the vegetable patch – it's excellent for getting vegetable seedlings off to a good start – and because it's richer than normal compost it goes much further.

Worms are so efficient at breaking the material down that they can get through at least their own weight in organic matter every day.

Worm bins are readily available from organic or vermicomposting suppliers. The bin that I have is a plastic tiered system that makes the compost very easy to harvest. You simply put your kitchen waste in the bottom layer, and the worms wriggle upwards to reach it. As the supply runs out, you add another tier with more bedding and waste, and the worms leave their casts behind in the lower tier, wriggling upwards once again in search of food. The system also collects excess liquid which is dispensed via a tap. This is a wonderful plant feed that can be used on pot plants, houseplants and vegetables while you are waiting for the next harvest of compost.

Making a wormery

As an alternative to a commercial plastic bin you could make your own wooden worm box (make sure the wood hasn't been treated with chemicals and treat it yourself with linseed oil or a non-chemical preservative). A simple box 30cm (12in) deep, 60cm (24in) wide and 90cm (36in) long should be about the right size for the quantities of kitchen waste produced by a family of four. Making the box shallow and long enables you to spread the waste out so that there is more surface area for the worms to nibble at. Construct a lid that can be taken on and off easily, and drill at least 12 holes in the base for aeration and drainage. Aeration is essential because worms need oxygen to survive. In addition, like standard composting, vermicomposting is an aerobic process, and the millions of microorganisms also at work in the box need good quantities of oxygen to work efficiently. Put your box wherever it is convenient – in the garage, outside in a shady spot, on a balcony, or even in your kitchen. When you have decided on a site, build a small platform for it with four bricks or blocks of wood, and position a tray underneath to collect the excess liquid. The worms thrive at temperatures of 18–25°C (64–77°F), so make sure the box isn't in full sun.

Setting up a wormery

The most important part of the wormery is the worms themselves. Don't go worm-hunting for big fat earthworms because they aren't the right type. The worms suitable for this kind of composting are the small red worms, *Eisenia foetida* (also known as tiger or brandling worms), which when you look closely have alternating bands of yellow and maroon down the length of their bodies. They are often seen in compost heaps and also in piles of animal manure, but never in normal garden soil because they need highly refined organic matter rather than a mineral-based medium to survive. A similar worm, *Lumbricus rubellus*, which can also be used for vermicomposting, is deep red without the yellow bands. It's best to buy worms from worm farms or organic suppliers as you will need large quantities – at least 2,000 – to start a worm bin.

Stackable plastic wormeries are widely available to buy, and make worm composting remarkably easy.

Some companies sell worms by mail order, which is how mine arrived. Remember to warn the rest of your family before the package lands on your doorstep!

The next step is to prepare the environment for your new guests. As well as regular supplies of kitchen waste, the worms need high-fibre bedding material, which, in time, will be eaten too. Bedding can be made from a number of materials. The cheapest and easiest is newspaper. Black and white newsprint is usually vegetable-based and non-toxic; avoid sections with coloured ink. Shred the newspaper into long, thin strips and add it in a layer that is 10–15cm (4–6in) thick. Partially decomposed shredded leaves are another good source of bedding, but avoid oak leaves as they can mat together and will take a long time to rot down. One of the best bedding materials is coir (coconut fibre). It is available in brick-sized blocks, which you pre-soak in a bucket of water. As it has excellent water retention properties, coir can sometimes be a little heavy on its own, so mix it with shredded newspaper for an excellent all-round bedding medium. Worms breathe through their skin, so the bedding must always be moist and aerated. The ideal moisture content is 75 percent, which is much more than the 50 percent of a normal compost heap, so soak any bedding thoroughly before putting the worms in.

Adding the worms
Get the worms into their new home as soon as possible, and start adding small amounts of kitchen scraps immediately, burying them in the bedding material in several spots

throughout the box. If the waste isn't buried, it may start to smell and can attract fruit flies or vermin. You can feed the worms almost every plant-based waste from your kitchen, but avoid raw potatoes and onion, which they don't seem to be very fond of, and too much citrus fruit, which can cause an overly acidic environment.

Most importantly, don't overfeed the worms. If they have too much to cope with, what they can't eat will start to rot down anaerobically (without oxygen). Anaerobic microorganisms give off gases that produce foul-smelling odours, and you end up with a wet, smelly mass. Feed small amounts at first and if they seem to be getting through it all, gradually increase the amounts.

Inspect your worm bin regularly. A sure sign of unhappy worms is when they are crawling away from the centre up the sides. This indicates that the bin may be too wet, too dry or too acidic for them, and if you don't do something about it, the worms will eventually die. Often, the addition of new bedding is enough to correct the imbalance, by providing a fresh environment towards which the worms can crawl. Dead worms don't need to be removed; their bodies are quickly decomposed by the other organisms in the bin.

Aftercare

Once you've set up the worm bin, provided you've created the right environment for them and are giving them the right quantities of food, the worms really won't need much attention apart from regular feeding. One further addition recommended by some vermicomposting experts is the occasional handful of powdered limestone (calcium carbonate), which prevents the conditions in the bin from becoming too acidic. Adding finely crushed eggshells will have similar results.

Unlike normal compost, vermicompost doesn't need turning because the worms do all the mixing for you. Moving through the compost looking for food, they mix and aerate the material, spreading other organisms through it as they go. They breed incredibly fast: from birth, a worm can reach sexual maturity in 4–6 weeks, and because they are hermaphrodites, all of them reproduce. The population of a wormery can double within a month, and would increase even faster if it weren't for the fact that many of the egg capsules and tiny thread-like hatchling worms are taken out when the compost is removed. As the population increases, you'll find you can also increase the amount of kitchen waste you feed them.

Harvesting the compost

After about three months, you'll be able to harvest your first worm compost. If you don't have a tiered system, the easiest way to do this is to move the pile of worm casts to one side in the bin, and then add fresh bedding on the empty side. Bury a handful or two of kitchen waste in the new bedding and, after a day or two, most of the worms will migrate over to the fresh bedding, leaving the pile of worm casts more or less empty and ready to scoop out. Some worm cocoons and tiny worms will be left, but enough worms will have moved to keep the population going.

Another way to harvest worm compost is to tip everything out into a heap on a large plastic sheet. The worms are sensitive to light and will burrow frantically downwards to get away from it, so you end up with tangles of slimy worms near the bottom and the worm casts on top. This method can take some time, and involves carefully scraping away the worm casts bit by bit, as the worms retreat further and further, eventually forming a tangled mass. Now all that remains is to grab handfuls of them and dump them back in the bin with new bedding and kitchen scraps to get them going again.

The resulting worm compost is not only extremely high in nutrients, it also has excellent structure, porosity, aeration and moisture-holding capacity – as a result of the worms' burrowing action – and contains very few pathogenic microorganisms, because most are destroyed in the worm's gut. On the whole it is finer and more friable than normal compost, making it excellent for seedlings in small quantities and for adding to potting mediums. It can also be used in much the same way as normal compost (see chapter 8), by digging it into your garden soil, or by using it as a mulch: because it is richer you won't need to use so much of it.

The benefits of worm composting

- A wormery is one of the best ways to compost kitchen scraps

- You can keep your worm bin on a balcony, in a garage or even in the kitchen

- Tiger worms can eat at least their own weight in organic matter every day, and they can double their population in a month if conditions are right

- Worm compost contains much more of the essential plant nutrients than normal soil

- Worm bins also produce excess liquid that can be used as a plant feed

Common problems

The environment you create for the worms has to be exactly right; if it is not, their lives may be in jeopardy. There are a few hazards that can throw a worm bin out of kilter.

Problem: The worm bin is too dry and the worms are inactive.

Solution: When you add food to the worm bin, check that the contents are moist. Sprinkle the bedding material with water if it's too dry. All worms need moisture, as they breathe through their skin, which has to be moist for the exchange of air to take place.

Problem: The worm bin is too wet and the worms seem to be dying.

Solution: Make sure that the drainage holes aren't blocked, and add dry bedding material to soak up the moisture. Some people suggest drawing off excess moisture with a turkey baster. Too much water reduces oxygen supplies and the worms will 'drown'.

Problem: The contents of the worm bin are too acidic and the worms are trying to escape up the sides.

Solution: Add powdered limestone or crushed eggshells to increase alkalinity. It can be difficult to tell if your worm bin is too acidic, but this can often be the cause of a worm population dying, and is particularly likely to occur if you have put in too much citrus fruit.

Problem: The bin is smelly and the worms have too much food.

Solution: Again, this is a common problem. Excess food can start to rot down anaerobically, making a smelly, rotting mass that is unpalatable to the worms. Eventually, the excess moisture created will kill them. Add kitchen waste in small amounts only, especially at first when the worm population hasn't yet had time to multiply. Increase the quantities gradually as time goes on.

Problem: The worm bin gets too hot or cold and the worms are sluggish or dying.

Solution: To make it cooler, position your worm bin in a shady place out of direct sunlight. In winter, insulate the box in some way – with bales of straw or bubble wrap, for example, or take it into a garage or shed. Tiger worms work most efficiently between temperatures of 10–25°C (50–77°F). Any hotter or colder than that and they tend to get sluggish; they may die in temperatures below freezing.

Using your compost

There's nothing quite like the satisfaction of filling a barrow with your very own dark, crumbly compost and digging it into the soil. It should make you feel good on so many levels: you have successfully recycled a significant amount of material that would probably have ended up in a landfill; you have created something out of materials that are otherwise regarded as useless; and you're helping to keep the soil healthy, so it in turn can feed the plants that feed you. So enjoy gardening with it, and of course use it wisely to get the best results.

When to use it

The optimum time to apply compost to the soil is in spring, two or three weeks before planting, but in fact there is no right or wrong time. Most people add it whenever they're digging over a free bed, particularly in autumn after the main growing season is over. If you're using it in spring, make sure that it is well rotted, otherwise nitrogen (an essential nutrient for plant growth) may be used up by the soil organisms working to decompose the half-rotted matter. If you're using it in autumn, it doesn't matter so much if it is not as well decomposed because by the time spring comes around the soil organisms will have done their work. If the compost is very rough, it can be sieved before use, particularly if you want it for seedlings or to make potting compost. Push it through a garden sieve and return the larger pieces of material back into the compost heap to continue rotting down.

There are no set rules as to how much compost to use on your beds as this is largely dictated by the amount you can produce, as well as the type of soil you have to start with. A poor quality clay soil will need much more compost – dug in over a period of several years – than a soil that already has reasonable structure, for example. In a vegetable garden, the amount of compost you apply to different beds will vary, because some crops are greedier than others and therefore need richer soil (see p. 84). As a general guide, apply a layer of at least 5cm (2in) over the entire surface area of your garden each year, to be dug in or used as a surface mulch. This roughly translates into one wheelbarrow load for an area of 5 by 5m (15 by 15ft). With worm compost, which is richer in nutrients, you can be more sparing.

Seedlings

Compost can be used to make a potting mixture for seeds, but use it in small amounts because its high chemical content can be detrimental to seedlings. Sieve it finely and mix it with equal parts of sand and good garden soil. Worm compost is especially good for seedlings because of its fine texture, but use it even more sparingly because of its even higher nutrient content. When transplanting seedlings, add a handful of compost to the planting hole to get the plants off to a good start in life. Seedlings that have been raised inside or in a greenhouse are susceptible to a fungal disease known as damping off, and compost can help to prevent this because of its resistance to disease pathogens.

The vegetable garden

All crops benefit from an application of compost; some need it more than others (see p.84). Not only do they need the nutrients that the compost makes available and the water it

Dig in plenty of compost with a fork, or lightly spread it over the surface and let the worms do the rest.

retains, but their roots benefit from being able to penetrate deeply into the crumbly textured soil that compost helps to create. If your soil needs building up, dig in a dose of compost in the autumn and then add more in spring, a few weeks before you sow seeds or transplant seedlings. Alternatively, it can simply be scattered on the surface of the soil or lightly raked in for the worms to take down.

In the vegetable garden compost can also be used as a mulch in spring: spread it out on the surface of the soil around each plant. A mulch conserves moisture and suppresses weeds, and a compost mulch has the added advantage of containing nutrients that slowly leach down into the soil when it rains. If your compost is in short supply, it can be used as a top-dressing on particular plants that look less healthy. Spread it in a circle around each plant, avoiding the stem. Remember that compost doesn't supply large amounts of nutrients at any one time, so you may need to supplement any additions of compost with an organic fertilizer.

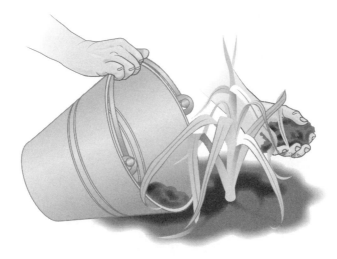

How much compost?

When growing vegetables it is advisable to follow the crop rotation principle, whereby crops are grouped according to type and nutrient requirement and are then grown together, but in a different site from year to year. This prevents a build up of soil-borne diseases and also ensures that the soil doesn't become depleted of certain minerals. Some groups of vegetables are classified as greedy feeders, needing as much compost as you can spare, others are less hungry, in which case adding too much compost can be detrimental.

Greedy feeders

The greedy feeders need lots of nitrogen and, therefore, plenty of compost. Members of this group are the brassicas (including cabbage, kale, cauliflower and broccoli), cucurbits (including courgettes, pumpkins and marrows) and solanaceous plants (potatoes, tomatoes, aubergine and peppers). Also in this group are sweetcorn, lettuce and other salad leaves.

Compost can be used in small amounts as a top dressing around plants that need a boost.

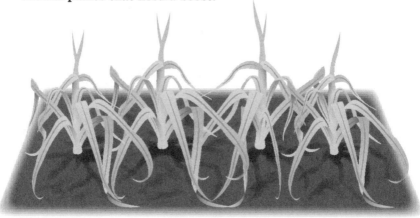

Light feeders

Members of this group don't need large amounts of organic matter, so use compost more sparingly. They include root crops (carrots, parsnips and turnips) and the alliums (onions, garlic, leeks and shallots).

Replenishers

This group covers the legumes (broad beans, runner beans, French beans and peas). Legumes 'fix' nitrogen from the air to replenish the soil, so don't need large amounts of nitrogen in the soil.

The flower garden

As with the vegetable patch, compost can be used on empty flower beds in autumn to build up the soil and restore its health. Either dig it in or spread it over the surface and cover it with an organic mulch such as chopped leaves or straw. In spring, it can be used as a mulch around annuals, perennials and shrubs. Roses are particularly grateful for a compost feed. When planting out potted plants or seedlings, add compost to the planting holes.

House plants

House plants are usually potted in a proprietory potting mix, but this can be supplemented with organic compost. Make your own potting mix with equal parts of loam, sand

and finely sieved compost. Old potting mixtures can be revived by adding compost to the surface and scratching it in around the plant.

To enhance the growth of a tree, rake compost into the soil around it, extending 30cm (12in) beyond the drip line.

Trees

Unlike other smaller plants, compost should not be used in the planting holes of large trees. This is because it will encourage the roots to stay inside the small area of the original hole rather than radiating outwards as they should do. Instead, compost can be spread in a ring around the tree, starting 60cm (24in) away from the trunk and extending 30cm (12in) beyond the tree's drip line (where its leaf canopy ends). Rake the compost in or dig it into shallow holes at regular intervals around the tree.

Lawns

An immaculate lawn needs a lot of work. When laying or sowing a new lawn, prepare the soil carefully first by working in as much compost as you can (heavy clay soils particularly benefit from this). The crumbly soil texture that it produces will promote good strong root growth, which is the key to a lush lawn. Once the lawn is established, its quality can be maintained by a yearly application of compost, finely sieved and scattered in a thin layer over the surface of the grass. It will soon be worked in by rain and worms.

Lawns will thrive if you give them a yearly application of finely sieved compost.

Compost tea

Compost tea is basically compost in a liquid form, and it can be used as a plant tonic for seedlings, young vegetables, flowers or pot plants. It offers the nutrition of compost but without the bulk. Recent research has shown that the use of compost teas can help to suppress diseases such as potato blight and mildew by controlling the pathogens that cause them. When sprayed onto leaves, beneficial organisms occupy the leaf surface, outnumbering the disease pathogens, so no infection can get in. Compost tea can also be used as a soil drench to develop a biological barrier around roots to help keep out the organisms that cause root disease.

There are many different ways to make compost tea. Two variations are described here. To make a simple compost tea, fill half a bucket with compost and top it up with water. Leave it to steep for a few days, then strain it through an old pair of tights or piece of sacking. To use, dilute to three parts water, one part tea, so that you end up with an amber liquid. Alternatively, put the compost in an old piece of sacking or burlap (or even an old pillow case), tie it at the top, and suspend it in a bucket or barrel. Leave it for several days, so that the nutrients leach out into the water and then dilute to use as before.

Make the most of it

Once you start generating large amounts of compost be sure to make the most of it. Although it may take a while for soil structure to improve and nutrient quantities to build up, the eventual benefits to the soil are enormous – and your plants will be living proof of this.

Once your compost is ready, make sure you use it. Nutrients can leach out if it is left for too long. It is best to store it under cover and use it within six months.

Once your compost is ready, make sure you use it. Nutrients can leach out if it is left for too long. It is best to store it under cover and use it within six months.

Tools of the trade

The only piece of equipment truly necessary for making compost is a good garden fork. A decent wheelbarrow helps too, in transporting material to be composted, and for moving the finished compost. However, for those taking the business of composting seriously, there are a few additional tools and items of machinery that help speed the process up and make life a bit easier.

Composting forks and aerators

If you find turning the heap difficult with your normal border fork, you can buy a special lightweight one designed specifically for compost making. These usually have a wider head than a standard fork, with

Special composting forks have long
handles and curved tines to make
turning the compost easier.

Compost aerators reduce the need to turn the heap regularly.

up to six tines. The tines are narrower and sometimes slightly curved, making it easier to mix the materials in your heap (and allegedly less detrimental to the creatures doing the work in there). Some companies also offer long-handled, lightweight forks for spreading the finished compost onto the soil.

Another hybrid composting tool is the compost aerator, which can be used instead of a fork to turn the mixture and inject oxygen into it. Aerators are particularly useful for those with bad backs. There are several variations on a theme, but most are made from steel or recycled plastic and usually have hinged 'wings' at the bottom. The wings fold down to be twisted within the pile; when the aerator is pulled out, they remain down, pulling the material out and creating new air passages. I have even come across an aerating tool that fits onto a hand drill. It is essentially a long spike with a corkscrew at the end – designed to take all effort out of aerating your compost.

Shredders

The most useful item for anyone with large amounts to compost (especially leaves or woody material) is a shredder.

As explained earlier, shredding helps to speed up the decomposition process by ensuring that more surface area is available to the worms, invertebrates and bacteria. Leaves, sticks, straw, ivy, brambles and tough old plants can all be run through a shredder before composting; some shredders can even be used for shredding finished compost to make it more uniform.

Shredders, powered either by electricity or petrol, are available from garden machinery manufacturers in many different forms and sizes. Electric shredders tend to be smaller than the petrol-powered machines, but are perfectly able to cope with everyday gardening debris. They are portable and lightweight and easier to turn on and off than petrol ones. Recently available is a new generation of 'quiet' electric shredders, handy for those who live in built–up urban areas. Generally more expensive than their electric counterparts, petrol shredders are heavy duty machines for large quantities of material. They are able to cope with quite substantial pieces of debris, including large branches.

Shredders are helpful if you have a large garden with lots of woody matter.

When choosing a shredder, make sure that you choose one that is appropriate for your needs. If you need to shred leaves and lawn clippings, you can opt for a less powerful machine than if you have piles of brambles and tree prunings, in which case you'll need something with a bit more oomph. The cutting device is just as important. Some shredders have rotating blades like a lawnmower, others have corkscrew-like mechanisms or steel hammermill devices. Blades can blunt very easily, so choose a model with replaceable blades so that you have one in use and one out for sharpening. Something else to look out for, particularly on the electric models, is the size of the entrance chute and the discharge vent: if these are too small, the machine may be liable to clog up frequently, especially if the material you are shredding isn't dry. Some electric machines have a handy cutter reverse switch to unclog the machine should this happen. The petrol shredders are larger and usually don't clog so easily, so from this point of view they are better if you want to shred wet or fibrous material.

Safety precautions with shredders

- Always wear protective glasses and gloves

- For noisier machines, also wear earplugs

- Wear long trousers and long sleeves in case of flying debris

- Keep your hands away from the entrance chute; coax material down with a stick

- Keep your hands away from the discharge vent

- Make sure children are well away from the action

Secateurs and loppers

If you decide not to invest in a shredder, material can be chopped with secateurs (sometimes known as pruners) or loppers. Yes, it takes a lot longer, but if you only have small amounts of waste to shred, cutting it up can be rather therapeutic. Invented in France in the nineteenth century, the first secateurs had precision-cut blades that scissored cleanly past each other in a 'bypass' action when the handles were squeezed. The design of bypass secateurs is essentially the same today, although they are highly refined and sophisticated in their twenty-first century forms. A slight variation is the 'anvil' action secateur, which has a single blade that cuts down onto a small plate and can be better for larger, tougher pieces of wood.

The blades of both types of secateur are made of steel – look out for hollow–ground steel blades (hand-ground to a concave shape at the base) as these are meant to be the best. Handles are made of carbon composite or aluminium and are usually cushioned for comfort. Some models feature a rotating action on the lower handle to help the cutting action.

Loppers are simply long-handled versions of secateurs. The long handles should help with leverage to cut the material more easily and may be more comfortable to use in preparing material for the compost heap. They too come in either bypass or anvil action, with tubular steel or aluminium handles, rubberized grips and strong steel blades.

Garden sieves or sifters

Another useful piece of kit for composting is a garden sieve or sifter, particularly if you need a fine-grade compost for seedlings or pots. Round brass sieves can be bought in sets, and there are modern steel, plastic or wooden versions, some with interchangeable screens of different-sized mesh. You can also use wooden battens and chicken wire or galvanized mesh to make your own sifter to fit over the top of a wheelbarrow, so that compost can be piled straight on top of it before being used in the garden. The larger pieces of compost that don't go through the sifter can be returned to the compost bin for further 'cooking'.

Garden sieves are useful if you want a fine-consistency compost.

Compost thermometers

Last but not least, for those who are determined to have all the accessories, there is the compost thermometer, used by keen composters to determine the optimum time to turn the heap (when the initial high temperatures have dropped slightly). Compost thermometers are usually made from non-corrosive steel with a large easy-to-read dial and a long spike to insert into the compost. Choose one that will reach at least 50cm (20in) into the heap.

Other ways to feed the soil

Composting is the most important part of organic gardening, but there are other ways to feed the soil, too. Based on the same principle of adding organic matter to the soil in some form or other, the following processes can be carried out in tandem with your normal composting routine; none are particularly time-consuming, and all can significantly benefit the soil and its plant life in the same way as compost.

Leaf mould

Leaf mould is a kind of refined compost, made with one ingredient only. If you have lots of trees in your garden, it's a good idea to make it in addition to compost: because leaves are so high in carbon they take a long time to rot down and this will slow down the rotting process in your compost heap. You may have to wait for up to two years for leaf mould – but the end result is a light, fibrous crumbly mixture that makes an excellent soil improver or potting compost mixture.

Almost any type of deciduous leaves can be added. Oak and plane leaves have a particularly high carbon content, so take longer than others to rot down – but they can still be used, as long as you are aware of this fact. Waxy leaves, such as holly, laurel and pine needles, also take ages to rot down, so should be used only in small quantities. Oak and beech leaves are more acidic than others, but become more alkaline as they decompose. Bear this in mind if you are using leaves from these trees only, and make sure the leaf mould is completely rotted before using it.

To make leaf mould, rake up the leaves as they fall in autumn, preferably just after it has rained so that the moisture content is reasonably high. To speed up the decomposing process, shred them – if you don't have a shredder, run over them with a lawnmower. Now, pile them together in a wire mesh bin made from four wooden posts and chicken wire, ideally 1m (3ft) high by 1m (3ft) wide so that the pile doesn't dry out. Place an old bit of carpet or a piece of plastic on top to keep out the rain. Alternatively, if you have a small garden that doesn't generate many leaves, leaf mould can be made in plastic dustbin liners with six or seven holes pierced in the bottom and sides for aeration and drainage. Tie the bag at the top when it is full.

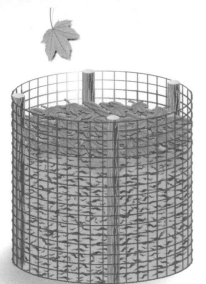

Made in a wire mesh container, leaf mould is particularly useful as a potting medium.

As you build the pile up, you can add a few handfuls of garden soil or finished compost in between the layers. This will speed up the process by introducing some soil organisms. Once you've made the heap, it will need very little attention other than a quick check every now and then to make sure it isn't drying out or getting too wet (if the moisture content is too high you can end up with a mushy mess). After a year or so, the leaves will have rotted down enough to make a rough mulch to be spread around vegetables, shrubs or perennials. After a year and a half to two years, the leaf mould should be fine and crumbly, and now makes an ideal potting medium for seeds, either used on its own or mixed with loam in equal parts. Tiny seedlings don't need a huge injection of nutrients – indeed too much nitrogen can be toxic – so for getting plants off to a good start, carbon-rich leaf mould is preferable to ordinary compost.

Green manures

I was confused by this term when I first heard it, probably because of the connotations of the word manure. Green manures are actually plants, grown for a season and then dug back into the soil to feed the plants that follow. They are particularly useful in vegetable plots, where patches of earth are left bare at times, particularly in winter.

Sowing a green manure crop is advantageous in several ways. Firstly, the crop covers the bare earth, protecting it from wind, rain and frost, which can cause erosion and damage to the soil structure. Below ground, the roots of the plants penetrate deep into the earth, helping to improve soil structure; above, the crop grows quickly over the earth, keeping weeds away. Perhaps most importantly, though, green manures can feed the soil. Most are nitrogen 'fixers', which means that they take nitrogen from the air and put it back into the soil. When they are dug in, the valuable nitrogen is made available to other plants that grow after them.

Growing a green manure crop is very easy. The seed is broadcast and gently raked in, and then the plants are left until they reach a certain stage of growth (usually just before flowering) or until the land is needed again, whichever is sooner. They are then dug back into the soil to rot down. Some hardy varieties are suitable for late summer and autumn planting, to be dug back in before planting seeds in spring; other less hardy, quick-growing varieties can be sown in spring and dug back in during the summer. The only thing to remember is not to leave the crop in the ground for too long. The longer you leave it, the tougher it will get and the more difficult it will be to dig it in – and even when it is dug in, under the ground, the soil organisms will find it tough going too, so decomposition will be slower.

Digging in
When digging in, turn the soil over, but don't bury the plants too deeply – no more than 15–20cm (6–8in) – because the

activity of the soil organisms may be inhibited by lack of air. If the plants are large, they can be scythed or chopped with a pair of shears before digging back in. Once dug in, wait a few weeks before planting new crops, because as the plant remains are decomposing, soil bacteria will be using extra reserves of nitrogen, which could be detrimental to a young plant in its first few weeks of life. In summer, when the soil is warm, the rate of decomposition is faster so you should only need to wait two weeks; in early spring, before the soil has had a chance to warm up, a gap of three to four weeks is recommended.

Green manure plants
For over-wintering
Alfafa (*Medicago sativa*) Deep-rooted, good for soil structure. Sow mid-spring to midsummer.

Winter field beans (*Vicia faba*) Good nitrogen fixer. Sow early to late autumn.

Phacelia (*Phacelia tanacetifolia*) Ferny foliage and blue flowers. Sow mid-spring to early autumn.

Winter tares (*Vicia sativa*) A swift-growing nitrogen fixer. Sow early spring to early autumn.

Trefoil (*Medicago lupulina*) Easy to grow. Sow mid-spring to late summer.

Grazing rye (*Secale cereale*) Extensive root system good for soil structure. Sow late summer to late autumn.

For spring or summer crops
Buckwheat (*Fagopyrum esculentum*) Attractive, deep-rooted plant. Sow early spring to midsummer.

Crimson clover (*Trifolium incarnatum*) Vigorous and swift-growing. Sow early spring to midsummer.
Fenugreek (*Trigonella foenum–graecum*) Swift-growing with lots of foliage. Sow early spring to midsummer.
Bitter lupin (*Lupinus angustifolius*) Very good nitrogen fixer. Sow early spring to early summer.

Comfrey: a natural fertilizer

If there is one plant that I can name as an all-round do-gooder, it is comfrey. I first learned about it when I started allotment gardening: each plot seemed to have at least one clump of this rather insignificant plant, and I soon found out why. Containing high percentages of nitrogen, calcium and especially potassium, comfrey is a swift-growing plant that can be used as a mulch, as a compost activator, as a liquid feed and even as an ingredient in potting mixes. The most common form, *Symphytum officinale*, can be found growing in the wild, usually by streams or rivers, but the variety most frequently cultivated is *S.* x *uplandicum*, or Russian comfrey. Russian comfrey is more suitable as a garden plant as it rarely sets seed; common comfrey tends to spread uncontrollably, so beware of growing it.

The goodness of comfrey is found in its leaves. Using long roots that reach down deep, it taps minerals from the subsoil and these are transferred into the leaves, which as a result are extremely high in potassium (5.86 percent, at least twice the amount in farmyard manure) and nitrogen (3.53 percent). They are also remarkably fibre-free, which means they rot down very quickly.

Easily grown from root offsets, Russian comfrey quickly forms sizeable clumps which can be pillaged three or four times a season for their rich harvest of leaves. Cut the leaves with shears or a scythe or pull them off – but use gloves because the leaves and stem are covered with tiny hairs that can prickle and irritate the skin.

Using comfrey

The uses of comfrey are numerous. It is a useful compost activator, adding an injection of nitrogen for the bacteria to get their teeth into. Tear the leaves and spread them in a layer in the heap or mix them with other carbon-rich materials so that the liquid formed as the leaves rot down is absorbed by the drier material.

It is quick and easy to make an invaluable liquid fertilizer from comfrey – this is a fantastically nutritious plant feed that is as good as any commercial organic fertilizer. The way I do it is to steep an armful of comfrey leaves in a bucket of water for three or four weeks, but you can also stack the leaves in a container with a hole in the bottom and let them decompose naturally (with this second method the liquid must be diluted with 10–20 parts of water before using). The only disadvantage with the comfrey soaked in water is that it smells revolting. The response from your plants will make it worth holding your breath for though. Some people swear that the unpleasant smell keeps the bugs away, too.

Comfrey tea can be watered around plants or sprayed on as a foliar feed. It is particularly useful for pot plants such as tomatoes and peppers that need lots of potassium, and can also be used as a general tonic for indoor and outdoor pot plants.

When planting seed potatoes or runner beans – both of which respond well to a potassium-rich soil – throw comfrey leaves into the bottom of the trenches. They can also be used as a mulch around crops that need extra nutrients. A final piece of advice, from the Henry Doubleday Research Association (Britain's leading organic research body), is to mix comfrey leaves between layers of partially rotted leaf mould to create a potting mix par excellence. The leaf mould, which is high in carbon, but not high in nutrients, is given an extra boost by the nutrient-rich comfrey liquid as the leaves rot down. The resulting potting mixture makes a very good general potting compost, but you may need to reduce the quantities of comfrey if you are using the mixture for seedlings.

Case studies

One of the great things about composting is that there isn't a 'right way' to do it. People have their own tried and tested methods. They use different materials and different containers, have different ideas on layering and turning, and argue about how hot the compost should get. But whatever the route taken to get there, the finished result is always the same. To show the variation in methods, here are four separate case studies.

Large-scale composting

The Chelsea Physic Garden in London is a three-acre garden open to the public during the summer months. An intensively cultivated garden, it contains many rare specimen plants and trees. Composting takes place in a special area at the bottom of the garden, in four large containers made from breeze blocks and wood. They are built directly onto bare soil, but the material is piled on top of inverted bread crates to help air circulation. The first bin is the largest (3m (10ft) wide by 2m (6ft) high) to accommodate the raw materials, which in their unrotted state take up the most space. The other three bins are smaller (2m/6ft wide by 2m/6ft high). There is also a separate bin for leaf mould, because the numerous trees in the garden generate too many leaves to add to the compost.

The gardeners have lots of space, so they are able to store the raw materials separately, building up a good volume before making the heap. They divide these materials up into 'green' and 'woody', shredding the dry woody material first in a large petrol-powered shredder. Green materials include grass clippings, soft weeds, green offcuts and waste from the kitchen. Woody material is plentiful, including shrubby prunings, tree prunings and old herbaceous plants. Once there is enough raw material, the heap is constructed in the largest container, with alternate layers of green and woody material. It is then covered with a tarpaulin to keep in the heat. Because the heap is built all in one go, it is steaming hot within a couple of days. The compost is left for six to eight weeks before it is turned into the next container. Then a new heap is started in its place with material that has been building up during that time. The heap is turned twice more until it reaches the last container. By this time, it should be almost ready to use. In summer, the finished compost is ready after six months; in winter, the process is slower because the outside temperatures are lower. The finished compost is used as a mulch, as well as being dug into the soil as a general soil conditioner. It is also used when planting container-grown plants.

Allotment composting, British Isles

Antonia Williams has a standard-sized allotment plot of 11 by 5m (35 by 15ft). She grows a wide range of vegetables using organic principles, and composting is an essential part of her gardening routine. At the end of her plot, she has created a small area, enclosed by low fencing, where she makes compost in a plastic compost container that she bought cheaply from the local council. Like a large, tapered dustbin, it has a lid, aeration holes and a sliding 'trap door' at the bottom to give access to finished compost. She also has a separate enclosure for woody material.

Much of the material for Antonia's compost comes from vegetable remains on the allotment. Old plants can sometimes be tough and woody, so she chops them up with a sharp garden knife before adding them to the compost. She builds the heap up slowly in layers rather than constructing it all in one go, which she finds impractical – kitchen waste starts to smell if it isn't mixed with drier material and she would need more space to stockpile her ingredients. However, she does make sure she always has supplies of woody material on hand to layer with the kitchen waste she brings from home. She also brings shredded leaves from the tree in her garden, which she stores in black plastic dustbin bags for a year or so before adding in small amounts to her compost. She is lucky to have access to free horse manure, which is delivered to the allotments every few weeks from nearby stables. This she stores in dustbin bags too, leaving it to rot down for at least six months before adding it in layers to the compost, also in small amounts. Antonia doesn't turn her compost, preferring to leave it to its own devices to rot down over time. The design of her bin is perfect for this no-hassle method because of the trap door at the bottom. As she removes ready compost from the bottom, more material can be added at the top in a constant cycle. From raw material to finished compost takes anything from six months to a year.

Antonia uses her compost at any time of year – whenever she has an empty bed. She spreads it over the top of the soil rather than digging it in, leaving the earthworms and other soil organisms to do the work.

Large-scale garden composting, Canada

Tom Dawson and his wife Donna have a garden of 9 by 15m (28 by 50ft) in Alberta. There is a small plot of grass surrounded by wide borders that are literally stuffed with different plants, including perennials, bulbs and shrubs. The garden itself generates plenty of material for the compost heap, so Tom composts in four plastic bins of 75cm (30in) square by 1.2m (4ft) high, with lids and access

doors at the bottom, using a rotational system.

All kitchen waste is composted – even in the middle of winter with temperatures often reaching −40°C (−40°F) when they have to dig out the compost heap from a thick layer of snow. In summer, dead-headings and grass clippings are added, while in autumn, cuttings and prunings from the garden are shredded using a large petrol-powered shredder. In addition, clippings from Donna's mother's garden nearby are also added, increasing the volume of the heap.

During the winter, which can last for many months, the decomposition process slows considerably, so at the first signs of spring, Tom empties out each of the bins in turn and, making a large pile on the ground, mixes all the materials together to prepare them to start 'cooking'. He then puts everything back into the bins, making sure that there are layers of wet and dry, green and brown materials. Each bin is at a different stage of decomposition, from bin one (early stages) to bin four (almost finished). Every three to five weeks during spring and summer, Tom assesses the compost in bin four. If it's ready, he takes it out, sifts it, and stores the finished compost in dustbins before using it in the garden. Bin three is then turned into bin four, bin two into bin three, and so on, so that in the process the contents of each are turned. He will have already started a pile of new ingredients waiting to go into the empty bin 1. While turning, Tom adds water if necessary, or a handful or two of soil to get the process going. Using this system, Tom has found he can have finished compost within 12 weeks.

An average yield each season is about 20 large bucketfuls of compost, which is used as a mulch around the plants and also dug into the soil when there is a free bed. The results show in the plants, which grow strongly and lushly throughout the spring and summer.

Small-scale garden composting, USA

Dean Riddle lives in the middle of the Catskill Mountains in upstate New York, USDA Zone 5. He has two small gardens near his cottage; one is a fenced kitchen and cutting garden of 6.5 by 9m (21½ by 28ft) and the other, 6.5 by 8.5m (21½ by 37¾ft), is surrounded by privet hedge and contains trees, shrubs and herbaceous borders. Dean has a low-maintenance compost heap that he simply piles on the ground without using a container, and another slow heap for woody material that takes a long time to rot down. To make the pile look neat he rakes the sides up so they don't sprawl.

Dean composts all his fruit and vegetable waste from the kitchen, plus all the garden rubbish. The kitchen garden, where mostly annual vegetables and flowers are grown, yields a lot of material at the end of the season when Dean cuts down and cleans up after the first frost. Every other year, in the autumn, he rebuilds the compost heap, making alternate layers of green and brown material, starting with a layer of sunflower stalks at the bottom for aeration, and watering as he goes. If he has animal manure, he will add this in too in layers, tossing in some lime here and there to add calcium. Once built, the heap isn't turned or watered. It is left for a year or so before the material at the bottom of the heap is ready to use; Dean simply collects it from the bottom as he needs it.

The compost is used as a mulch in spring and early summer, after Dean has done all the major planting and the self-sown plants are up to a good size. He mulches all the beds with 10cm (4in) of compost, trying to do it after a good rain and before the soil has had a chance to bake. He also uses his compost when planting out annuals and perennials, and adds it to his potting mix for containers. When visitors admire his self-sown plants (such as *Verbena bonariensis*, red orach and white cleome), he offers them a bag of his compost because he knows it will be full of the seeds. The pile doesn't reach high enough temperatures to kill off the seeds, so Dean is careful not to put gone-to-seed weeds in it.

Conclusion

The case studies in the previous chapter provide just a few examples of how people can adapt the basic methods of composting to their own needs and resources. They demonstrate the flexibility of the process, and the variety of uses compost can be put to in the garden. I'd also like to think that they show how relaxed people can be about it! Dean's low maintenance heap in the last case study is something that anyone can do with minimal effort.

I hope that this book will open a few people's eyes to the natural processes that make composting happen. With this understanding, I guarantee you'll look at the compost heap in a new light, full of awe for all the unseen work that is going on in there. You'll be better equipped to produce the kind of compost your plants love, your garden will flourish and you can also feel proud that you are recycling more of your waste, thereby helping the environment. And although your garden might be private property, it won't be yours forever, so look at it as an investment for future generations – feeding the soil so that it in turn feeds us. Rather than nipping down to the garden centre next time you need a soil improver, think long term. Start building a compost heap today and in 12 month's time you'll be reaping the benefits. What are you waiting for?

Further information

Glossary

Actinomycetes: Species of fungi in the decomposition process noted for their branching, cobwebby growth pattern. Some species have antibiotic properties.

Aerobic: Requiring available oxygen to live. Composting is an aerobic process – requiring oxygen to take place.

Aggregates: Comparatively large particles formed from individual soil particles of clay, sand and silt, bound together by humus.

Allotment: An area of publicly owned land divided into plots. The plots are rented out, usually specifically for growing vegetables.

Anaerobic: The opposite of aerobic. Anaerobic decomposition takes place if air is excluded.

Cellulose: The 'woody' substance that is the main constituent of plant cell walls. Plants high in carbon contain a large proportion of cellulose.

Coir: Coconut fibre, often used for bedding in worm bins, also found as an alternative to peat in potting composts.

Community composting: Composting on a large scale, utilizing the green waste of a local community to make bigger amounts of compost.

Comfrey: An easy-to-grow plant whose leaves are especially high in potassium and nitrogen. Can be used as a mulch, compost activator or liquid plant feed.

Compost: Decomposed organic matter; the man-made form of humus. The word derives from the Latin *componere*, to combine. Compost may also refer to a purchased soil mix (potting compost).

Compost activator: A substance that speeds up the process of decomposition. Commercial compost activators contain dormant bacteria that are stimulated when water is added.

Compost tea: A liquid plant feed made by steeping quantities of compost in water.

Crumb structure: A term used to describe the texture and composition of the soil.

Damping off: A usually fatal fungal disease affecting seedlings. The stem is infected at soil level and collapses.

Decomposer: An organism that contributes to the decomposition process by breaking down the cells of dead plants and animals into simpler substances.

Fertilizer: A natural or artificial substance containing the chemical elements that improve plant growth and productivity.

Green manure: A plant that is grown for a season and then dug back into the soil to enrich it. Often green manure plants have the ability to 'fix' nitrogen from the air and therefore they provide a good source of nitrogen for the plants that are grown in the same site afterwards.

Hard pan: A hard crust that forms on the surface of the soil, particularly clay soils.

Hermaphrodite: A term for an organism that possesses both male and female sex organs. Most worms are hermaphrodites.

Humus: Decomposed organic matter; a dark brown substance in the soil resulting from the natural decomposition of organic matter.

Leaching: The washing out or down of nutrients or chemicals by water.

Leaf mould: Decomposed leaf matter, an excellent soil improver.

Legume: Any member of the pea family.

Loam: A generally fertile and balanced soil, containing sand, clay, silt and a significant amount of organic matter.

Macroorganism: An organism that can be seen without the need for magnification.

Manure: A fertilizer that is mixed into the soil to enrich it. In modern-day usage it often refers only to animal dung, but its original meaning was broader.

Mesophiles: Species of bacteria that survive at mid-temperatures during the decomposition process.

Microorganisms: Microscopic organisms such as bacteria, protozoa or fungi. Sometimes known as microbes.

Mulch: A layer of organic or inorganic material placed on the soil to conserve moisture and warmth, suppress weeds and, in the case of an organic mulch, to provide nutrients that leach down into the soil.

Nitrates: The chemical forms of nitrogen that are available to plants.

Nitrogen fixers: A term applied to plants (such as green manures) that are able to obtain nitrogen from the air, rather than the soil. Having 'fixed' nitrogen from the air, these plants are rich in nitrogen and are useful for digging back into the soil to enrich it.

Perlite: A white soil additive derived from volcanic materials.

Pressure-treated: A process of treating wood with chemicals to preserve them.

Protozoa: Single-celled microscopic organisms.

Psychrophiles: Species of bacteria at work early on in the decomposition process, at low temperatures.

Soil conditioner: A substance that improves the texture of the soil.

Streptomycetes: In the same group of fungi as actino-mycetes, noted for their branching, cobwebby growth pattern. Some species have antibiotic properties.

Thermophiles: Species of bacteria that work at the hottest temperatures.

Windrow: A specially shaped, elongated compost heap, mainly used for large-scale composting.

Vermicompost: Compost produced by worms.

Vermiculite: A soil additive derived from a mineral called mica.

Useful addresses

British Isles
The Centre for Alternative Technology
Machynlleth,
Powys SY20 9AZ
Tel: +44 (0) 1654 702400
Email: help@catinfo.demon.co.uk
info@cat.org.uk
Website: www.cat.org.uk

The Composting Association
Avon House
Tithe Barn Road
Wellingborough
Northamptonshire NN8 1DH
Tel: +44 (0) 1933 227777
Email: membership@compost.org.uk
Website: www.compost.org.uk

Federation of City Farms and Community Gardens
The Greenhouse
Hereford Street
Bristol BS3 4NA
Tel +44 (0) 117 923 1800
Website: www.farmgarden.org.uk

Henry Doubleday Research Association (HDRA)
Ryton Organic Gardens
Coventry CV8 3LG
Tel: +44 (0) 24 7630 3517
Website: www.hdra.org.uk

Soil Association
Bristol House
40–56 Victoria Street
Bristol BS1 6BY
Tel: +44 (0) 117 929 0661
Email: info@soilassociation.org
Website: www.soilassociation.org

Waste Watch
96 Tooley Street
London SE1 2TH
Tel: +44 (0) 870 243 0136
Website: www.wastewatch.org.uk

North America and Canada
City Farmer
Canada's Office of Urban Agriculture
801–318 Homer Street
Vancouver
British Columbia V6B 2V3
Tel: +00 1 604 685 5832
Email: cityfarm@interchange.ubc.ca
Website: www.cityfarmer.org

The Composting Council of Canada
16 Northumberland Street
Toronto
Ontario M6H 1P7
Canada
Tel: +00 1 416 535 0240
Email: info@compost.org
Website: www.compost.org

Cornell University Composting
Cornell Waste Management Institute
Cooperative Extension
152 Riley-Robb Hall
Ithaca, NY 14853–5701
Tel: +00 1 607 255 7654
Email: nraes@cornell.edu

The Rodale Institute
611 Siegfriedale Rd
Kutztown PA 19530
Tel: +00 1 610 683 1400
Email: info@rodaleinst.org

US Composting Council
1924 N. Second Street
Harrisburg PA 17102
Tel: +00 1 631 864 2567
Email: info@compostingcouncil.org
Website: www.compostingcouncil.org

Where to buy compost bins

British Isles
The Organic Gardening Catalogue
Riverdene Business Park
Molesey Road
Hersham
Surrey KT12 4RG
Tel +44 (0) 1932 253666
Email: chaseorg@aol.com
Website: www.organiccatalog.com

Queenswood Garden Products
Wellington
Hereford HR4 8BB
Tel: +44 (0) 1432 830015
Email: sales@queenswood.co.uk
Website: www.queenswood.co.uk

North America and Canada
Composters.com
PO Box 1684
Laguna Beach, CA 92652
Tel: +00 1 800 233 8438
Email: staff@composters.com
Website: www.composters.com

Greenline Products
1280 Finch Avenue West, Ste 413
North York
Toronto
Ontario M3J 3K6
Canada
Tel: +00 1 416 667 9396

W. Atlee Burpee
300 Park Avenue
Warminster
PA 18974
Tel: +00 1 800 333 5808
Email: burpeecs@surfnetwork.net
Website: www.burpee.com

Gardener's Supply Company
128 Intervale Road
Burlington
VT 05401
Tel: +00 1 800 833 1412
Email: info@gardeners.com
Website: www.vg.com

Smith & Hawken
25 Corte Madera
Mill Valley
CA 94941
Tel: +00 1 800 940 1170
Website: www.smithandhawken.com

Worm composting

Green Gardener
41 Strumpshaw Road
Brundall
Norfolk NR13 5PG
Tel: +44 (0)1603 716986
Website: www.greengardener.co.uk

Wiggly Wigglers
Lower Blakemere Farm
Blakemere
Herefordshire HR2 99X
Tel: 0800 216990/ +44 (0)1981 500391
Website: www.wigglywigglers.co.uk

All Things Organic
471 Pemberton Terrace
Kamloops
British Columbia V2C 1TC
Canada
Tel: +00 1 250 372 1835
Email: info@allthingsorganic.com

Useful websites

The Rot Web: www.a-horizon.com

The Compost Resource Page: www.oldgrowth.org

The Master Composter: www.mastercomposter.com

Mary Appelhof's site for worm composting resources: www.wormwoman.com

Index

About the Author

Clare Foster is Editor of *Gardens Illustrated* magazine, which has been dubbed 'the *Vogue* of garden magazines'. She is the author of two previous books, *From Bud to Seed: Perennials* and *From Bud to Seed: Annuals* (Conran Octopus 2001) and writes regularly for *Gardens Illustrated* on topics ranging from kitchen gardens to garden design. She learned about making compost by talking to people on her allotment in West London, where she grows her own organic vegetables.